SUCCESSFUL
DUCK
HUNTING

M.D. JOHNSON
Photos by Julia Johnson

Published by

 **krause publications**

Please call for our free catalog. Our toll-free number to place an order or obtain a free catalog is 800-258-0929 or please use our regular business telephone 715-445-2214 .

Library of Congress Catalog Number: 2001088590
ISBN: 0-87349-215-3
Printed in the United States of America

Dedication

To Pop – for the love of the outdoors; to Ma – for the love of the language; to Julie – for turning 'I can't' into 'I did' … and 'I do'; and to Maggie, history's finest free duck dog.

Foreword

Some evening next fall, M.D. Johnson will call me. With no preamble, he'll get right to the point: "I've got both boats and three dozen decoys loaded in the back of my truck. Meet me at Babcock at 6:00 tomorrow morning. All you need to bring is your shotgun." And no matter what I had planned for the next day, I'll put it off, because a morning spent hunting ducks with a waterfowler as passionate and exuberant as M.D. Johnson always rekindles my own enthusiasm for the hard work of sleet-in-the-face, hide-in-the-mud, freelance waterfowling.

If we're meeting at 6:00 a.m. and I roll up at 5:59, I can guarantee that M.D. will have already dragged both Aquapods down to the water's edge. He'll have loaded the boats with two of everything and will be pacing the shore, impatient as a kid at Christmas waiting for his parents to wake up.

That M.D. will get us into ducks goes without saying. If there are ducks to find, M.D. will have found them and plotted a scheme to get at them — like the day last fall when we towed his sneakboats along a bare shoreline, then layed out in the sparsest, shortest cover imaginable, limiting on greenheads and greenwings who had rafted in the spot precisely because there was no place for a hunter to hide.

So of course, we'll kill birds, and M.D. will derive more pleasure from watching me shoot a duck than in shooting one himself. More important, M.D. won't let me forget to watch the sun rise, to listen to the sights and sounds of the marsh, and to laugh a lot.

The traits that make M.D. Johnson a delight to hunt with render him eminently qualified to write the book you hold in your hands. *Successful Duck Hunting: A Look into the Heart of Waterfowling* is the product of 26 full duck seasons spent hunting rivers, ponds, marshes and fields from Ohio to Washington state. In that time, M.D. has mastered the how-to of waterfowling — from scouting to making a jerk string — as well as anyone. He may be the best (certainly he's the most fanatical) I've ever seen when it comes to hiding from ducks.

Expert though he may be, M.D. knows waterfowling is a matter of life and death only to the ducks, not to us, and he can take a joke at his own expense when the birds won't do his bidding. I remember watching M.D. call to some ducks who gave him a collective cold shoulder. "I suck at this," he laughed, as the flock shrank into black specks in the distance.

"M.D., You're supposed to blow," I told him.

Now M.D. blows a call better than most of us, but he's not afraid to defer to the likes of well-known waterfowlers Buck Gardner and Phil Robertson, both of whom he interviewed for the chapters on calling. Similarly, he tapped the expertise of Mississippi river guide Tony Toye for his chapter on hunting big rivers. You'll even find me quoted in the shotgun chapter, although having seen M.D. double on greenwings and triple on bluewings, I can tell you he doesn't need my advice on shotgunning.

There's another M.D. Johnson aside from the M.D. who makes a day in the marsh so much fun. It's the M.D. who shoots from the lip (and the heart), firing off e-mail screeds that light up my computer screen, angrily lamenting the direction he fears waterfowling is headed. M.D. is an unabashedly low-tech, low-budget traditionalist who believes that high-dollar leases, battery operated decoys, and expensive gear and gadgets take us farther and farther away from the essence of the sport. Don't expect doom and gloom in this book, however, just be aware that M.D. would rather hunker in the cattails than sip coffee in a heated blind at a private club. Recognize, too, that the tips and techniques M.D. offers in this book have been tried and proven in the real world of blue-collar, public land waterfowling.

Turn to chapter one. M.D. Johnson is waiting inside. He's got boats loaded, the decoys bagged and he's eager to take you along. I know you'll enjoy spending time with him as much as I do.

Phil Bourjaily
Shooting Editor, *Field & Stream* magazine
Iowa City, IA
February, 2001

Acknowledgements

Very little in life is accomplished as the result of a solo effort. This book, and most importantly, the lifetime of outdoor education that supplied the foundation and research base for it, is certainly no exception. With that in mind, I'd like to take the opportunity – sounds like the intro for a Grammy Award acceptance speech, eh? – to thank the folks who actually made this possible. These are the folks who opened the doors, who said "Just try it one more time," and who showed me a thousand different sunrises over a thousand different decoy spreads. This is *your* book.

To the dozens of waterfowlers coast to coast who took the time to share with me their expertise; to Chip Gross and Bob "Greenie" Grewell, for the advice and the encouragement to continue in the wonderful world of outdoor writing despite the many setbacks; to the manufacturers and outfitters without whose help, time, and guidance this book – and a bulk of my waterfowling career – wouldn't have been possible; to Buck Gardner, for his one-on-one duck calling lesson; to Bob Wolfe, Eunice Peck (1899-1979), and Elmer Simmons (1908-2000), who owned the swamps where I grew up; to Dave Fountain, for revealing the "secret of the lagoons"; to Tony "The Jakeman" Miller, for constantly reminding me that duck hunting is supposed to be fun…and for making me laugh. And to my wife and constant field companion, Julie, whose talents behind a camera allowed visions that would have been impossible to put into words, and whose love, encouragement, and support made this project possible…and made the whole of this old waterfowler's world a much, much better sunrise. Love you.

And to everyone else who's shivered or sweated alongside me in a blind, thanks for the company.

Table of Contents

Introduction

Random Thoughts Before Getting Started

I shot my first duck when I was 10, a little kid with a too-big gun wearing a too-big Elmer Fudd hat draped in a way-too-big hunting coat that my mother constantly assured me I would grow into. Growing into things, back in 1974, was slow then; especially in Newton Falls, a small 'burg in the northeastern corner of Ohio whose only claim to fame was her zip code – 44444, and who, 26 years later, hasn't shaken off her claim as a "wonderful town to grow up in."

The bird was a hen mallard. A one-legged hen mallard. My father, a biology teacher, explained to me that she had in all likelihood been born that way. This evaluation came after a thorough swamp-side examination of both the duck and her missing appendage. As for me, I didn't care that the duck – "my" duck – had only one leg, nor did I care that the reason behind me having my first-ever duck had nothing, absolutely nothing, to do with shotgunning skills or accuracy. It didn't matter that this duck had been the result of the mallard's unfortunate in-flight rendezvous with an ounce and an eighth of lead fours hastily thrown in what only could be described as a general direction. What I cared about was that I was now a duck hunter, just like my dad.

The year before, ages it seemed, I'd been a duck shootist. I remember my father, one of history's finest deadpan — yet still waiting at the age of 61 to be discovered — comedians, telling a friend that I was the only person he knew of who could make a single-shot Harrington & Richardson 20-gauge sound as though it were belt-fed. In those days, I didn't hit many ducks. In fact, I didn't hit *any* duck; still I was adhering to Stage One in the Five Stages of the Hunter – that being the condition that the quality of a hunt is judged solely on the amount of shooting that takes place. Needless to say, most of my hunts were absolutely stellar successes. Truth be known, I put several of the Winchester and Remington kids through both private school and six years of college with the money my father spent on ammunition. But, hey, I was 9. Oh, and it didn't hurt any that my Babi and Dzedo – that's Czech for Grandma and Grandpa – owned a sporting goods store. Babi was pretty quick with the grandson discounts on ammunition.

Life back then was a hell of a lot simpler. I'm not talking about the bills or the mortgage or the long and seemingly ever-growing list of world problems that we can't help but be exposed to on a daily basis. No, I'm saying that things were just easier then. I remember a time when my biggest worry, the highest hurdle in my tiny world, was when I'd be big enough to walk out to The Muskrat House – not just any muskrat house, mind you, but "The" muskrat house – in Wolfe's Swamp, a landmark elementally named yet holding such significance in our waterfowling circle as to compete with the Space Needle and Las Vegas, both places I would visit later in life, and not enjoy nearly as much nor remember as fondly.

This was the place to sit, the epicenter of duck hunting as my father and his brother-in-law, Neal, knew it. A natural blind unlike any other. And so The Muskrat House became my brass ring, my personal Holy Grail. My reason, at the ripe old age of 10, for living. Unfortunately, two foot of legs – as my father used to say – and three feet of water just didn't work too well. Still don't in his opinion.

So I was carried; piggy-backed like a trapper's basket. Borne on my father's back like a sultan in his lofty man-powered conveyance; a 16-gauge Winchester Model 24 double in one hand, and a Remington 1100 in the other, and placed upon one of the most royal, albeit wild rose and willow-draped, thrones ever known. I'd made it. I'd reached Nirvana and it was this pile of sticks and cattails. I was there. I was at The Muskrat House. I didn't have to kill any ducks, though over the next two or three years, I did. No, I didn't have to do anything but sit and watch and listen. I was a duck hunter now.

It's funny the things that you learn, the bonds that are formed, when you're carried on the back and by the shoulders of another. It's real possible that at the time, my father, despite his two degrees and a Phi Beta Kappa key (I'm awful proud of both my folks), didn't realize fully, if at all, what he was doing by carrying me into Wolfe's Swamp. What he did, I've discovered over time, was open a door. He paved a way into a world that relatively few have seen, and even fewer have taken the time to appreciate to its fullest – the world of the waterfowler. It's a world of magic and of wonder. A place of indescribable things, each image elusive even to most accomplished poet, photographer, and wordsmith. And it's with this knowledge that I feel almost unworthy as I attempt to paint a picture of something that very possibly can't be shown in its entirety, but rather in brief tantalizing clips and segments. Still, I'd like to try.

Successful Duck Hunting: A Look Into The Heart Of Waterfowling does just what the title implies, for it provides a glimpse – sometimes in sharp focus, at other times, well, a little cloudy around the edges – into the world of the duck hunter. It's a chance to learn from some of the greatest outdoorsmen in the sport, folks such as World Champion and Champion of Champions duck caller, Buck Gardner ("You just put that call to your lips like you're takin' a drink out of a Coca-Cola bottle"), and Phil "The Duck Commander" Robertson, an incredibly modest duck hunting guru, though you won't hear him call himself that, whose reputation, talent, and what-you-see-is-what-you-get attitude is fast earning him a following which can only be described as cult-like. It's learning without knowing you're being taught. It's "Hey, why didn't I think of that?" My goal in writing *Successful Duck Hunting* was to find and present a mix of both education and plain, old-fashioned storytelling, all as seen through the men and women who have at the very core of their existence the North wind, the flyways, and the secrets that only waterfowlers share. Hopefully, when you're through and you've set the book aside, you'll find yourself a better waterfowl hunter. And, maybe, a better person.

But, too, it's a chance, to recognize and thank the very special people who have welcomed me and mine into their world, and allowed me to share their coffee, their kindness, their camaraderie, and their knowledge. This is also the chance to thank them for not being afraid, despite and perhaps in some cases because of their role as a male, to be human. It's a chance to wax poetic; to eulogize; to remember and reflect.

So, then, to everyone involved over the past 26 years, and most of you know exactly who you are and if you don't, you will, thank you for everything. This is for you and yours. It's because of you. I hope I don't disappoint you. And to my Babi and Dzedo, thanks for the shells. I'm doing well, but I miss you both.

M.D. Johnson
March 2001

1
Meet The Players

A bird's shape, even in silhouette, can give clues as to the species. The long tails identify many of these ducks as pintails or sprig.

A s Jim Schoby told it, it was indeed a day for the books. Not only had his shooting partner bagged the albino mallard flying with the group of regularly colored birds, but on retrieving his prize – he beat the dog to the downed bird – he discovered it was banded.

"The guy was beside himself," he said, his coffee cup hovering over his lips. An incredible storyteller, Schoby had a way of dragging you to the edge of your seat, and then throwing you right out of it.

"So he gets this thing back to the blind, all out of breath, and he starts looking it over. 'This is going to the taxidermist,' he's saying. Then he starts looking at the band. Looking at it close," Schoby said. "Know what it said? 'Property of Walt Disney World.'"

Schoby laughed so hard his eyes watered, despite the two decades that had passed since the hunt took place. Jim's gone now – a heart attack at age 53 while walleye fishing on Lake Erie. According to his boy, Jim Jr., Schob's passing couldn't have happened at a better place. Another time perhaps, but not a better place, save,

9

Cloudy days can make duck identification difficult; however, there was no mistaking this big drake mallard.

as the old man was always so fond of saying, "a duck blind on the Scioto River." Still, his albino mallard story, the one in which his hunting partner bagged Donald Duck, will never grow old.

Albino mallards, just like white deer, are rare things. In most cases, a duck hunter will live his entire life and never see a wild white mallard, instead having to settle for the traditional chestnut brown front, slate gray back, and namesake green head shown by 99.999 percent of

the nation's mallard population.

Because of their familiar colors, as well as their national distribution, mallards are among one of the most easily recognized waterfowl species in the United States; however, there are several species which aren't as readily identifiable. Sometimes the confusion or mystery as to "what duck was that" stems from the fact that not all species are found in all four major flyways, a subject which will be discussed in greater detail in Chapter 2.

America's most common and recognized duck, the drake mallard.

Others, like the brightly colored harlequin duck, simply aren't that common, or as is the case with the harlequin, are found only in certain parts of one or two flyways, and therefore aren't seen by hunters not living or hunting in that particular region.

But some might ask why, given the specific number of birds permitted by law in the daily bag limit, is waterfowl identification of any importance? First of all, and while bag limits may and often do differ between flyways, all bag limits restrict hunters to the harvest of a certain number of certain species. For instance, the limit on pintails, also known as sprig, in the state of Washington in any given season may be one per day; however, the daily bag may include seven ducks. Once that pintail is added to the bag, no more pintails may be taken that day, thus making the identification of individual birds *before* the shooting starts something of considerable importance. To further muddle things, some species – mallards, for example – require hunters to not only make an accurate identification as to the kind of duck, but also as to the sex of the bird. Again, whereas the state of Washington allowed hunters to take seven mallards as part of their daily bag limit in 2000, only two of those mallards could be females. Fortunately, under most conditions, there's very little that's difficult in differentiating between the mallard sexes; however, variables such as lighting, cloud cover, and plumage differences can all play a part in determining the sex of a bird, particularly one in flight.

Aside from the legal considerations, there are other reasons behind proper and accurate waterfowl identification. Tablefare, how good a certain species of duck tastes

on the table, is one reason to know what you're shooting at. Mallards, with their diet of grains and plant material, are considered by many to rank among the top three ducks in terms of taste. Likewise, the acorn-eating wood duck and the diminutive green-wing teal are also tasty birds. Conversely, birds whose diets consist primarily of animal matter, fish being the most notable and least desired, rate rather low on the "what's for dinner" scale. Such ducks would include mergansers, also known as fish ducks, shovelers, and several of the diving and seagoing waterfowl. Still, there are those whose palates are accustomed to that taste of these species, and many of these will claim to have secret recipes guaranteed to make even the toughest, fishiest merganser or coot a feast fit for a king – or at the very least, a mother-in-law.

With that, the question then turns to how one learns to identify a mallard from a merganser, or a blue-wing teal from a green-wing teal. Waterfowl identification might be best thought of as an on-going education, a course in sight and recognition, and one which can only be bettered through practice, repetition, book-learning, and, of course, more practice. Fortunately, there are several characteristics that all ducks share—although many of these elements can and will differ from time to time— that make identifying the different species a much less challenging task.

At this point, it's probably best to introduce and discuss the two basic types of ducks that hunters in the United States will most often encounter. These are the puddle ducks, also known as the puddlers or dabblers, and the diving ducks, commonly referred to simply as divers. Below is a list which spotlights those characteris-

Size and habitat both can provide information that will help answer the question, "What duck is that?"

tics, physical and otherwise, that set the one group apart from the others.

Puddle Ducks	Diving Ducks
Legs placed at middle of body	Legs set back toward tail
Walks easily on dry land	Awkward on land
Tips up to feed	Dives to feed
Feet smaller; small hind toe	Feet large, with large hind toe
Primarily found on shallow water	Deep-water habitat
Leaps into air directly from water	Running take-off
Moderate wingbeat	Fast wingbeat

It's important for you to remember that these guidelines are just that – guidelines, While each of these characteristics or clues are relatively universal and accepted, there are exceptions. Ringnecks, for instance, are classified as diving ducks, and yet will often share the same shallow-water habitat with mallards, widgeon, wood ducks, and other puddlers. Conversely, widgeon will often be found in the company of diving ducks such as canvasbacks, redheads, and scaup, where they rightfully earn their less-than-pleasant nickname, robbers, from their habit of stealing deep-water delicacies such as eelgrass or mussels from the more adapt divers once the divers have returned to the surface with their prize.

There is a third category into which several different species of ducks fall, one that for simplicity's sake we'll refer to it as "other." These are the fish ducks, the tree ducks, and the sea ducks. The category includes such species as the mergansers, scoters, fulvous and whistling tree ducks, old squaw, eiders, and goldeneye, as well as a handful of, there's that word again, others. Some of these, the mergansers for instance, show traits similar to those of the divers; however, and as always there's an exception, the hooded merganser is a cavity nester (as are both the common and Barrow's goldeneye) that can often be found on small woodland ponds more suited, perhaps, to wood ducks than any of the diving duck clan. Again, the categories and listed characteristics serve mainly as guidelines for identification purposes.

Where a particular duck is seen, what it eats, and how it acts are all good identification clues. There are, however, several other things that you can use to help identify a certain species. Among these are shape, size, color, wingbeat, speed of flight, flight style, and flock habits.

Size and shape both play major roles in identification, not so much between dabblers and divers, but, once that variable is determined, size allows for differentiation between members of the same group. Big ducks are big ducks, and would include mallards, pintails, and gadwalls on the puddler side, and canvasbacks, redheads, and the chunky scoters on the diver and sea duck side. Widgeon, ringnecks, and wood ducks would all be considered medium-sized by most hunters, while the teals, buffleheads, and perhaps even the shovelers would fall into the small category. A duck's shape, too, can be a use-

Color, like the blues and whites on this drake mallard's speculum, are good indicators.

ful tool in determining who's who. Puddle ducks are often seen as rounded, fuller birds, while divers will appear more streamlined; not surprisingly, there are exceptions, as the dabbling pintails are very streamlined, while the diving scaup and the tiny bufflehead, also known as the butterball, can and often are rather rotund.

Wingbeat, speed of flight, and flock habits are other give-aways. With their twisting, turning shorebird-like flight patterns, knot-tight flocks, and speed of light quickness, groups of teal are relatively easy to identify on the wing. In contrast, mergansers will often fly just over the water and in a single file line. Widgeon and gadwall, on the other hand, frequently appear as loose, almost dis-organized groupings, while canvasbacks and pintails both will seem to fly with fighter-pilot precision and coordination. Both while on the wing and on the water, color, color patterns, and color location can provide important information as to a duck's identify. A pale blue shoulder patch immediately points to either the small blue-wing teal or the slightly larger northern shoveler. A white speculum, that part of the wing farthest from the shoulder and also known as the secondary feathers, can only mean a gadwall – the only North American puddle duck marked as such. A red head? Here, you're looking at either a redhead or a canvasback; however, if a second look reveals a large bird with a long, sloping bill, that's a sure sign that the bird in question is indeed a canvasback.

Typically, coloration – and I'll single this variable out here for just a minute – is one of the best identifiers when it comes to telling one duck from another; however, there are times when separating the drakes from the hens visually can be difficult if not impossible. Twice each year, ducks will molt their body feathers. During this time and immediately after, a period known as the eclipse, the drakes of each species will very closely resemble the hens. This eclipse phase can last well into the start of the hunting season, with some species such as teal, not attaining their full plumage until most have reached their wintering grounds in the southern United States, Mexico, and central America. Juvenile or young drakes, those which haven't yet become fully feathered, can also appear drab and hen-like – the molt or eclipse phase notwithstanding. In many cases, eclipse or young drakes can only be identified through very close, if not in-hand examination. More than one hunter has been unpleasantly surprised to find – or rather, the local con-servation officer has informed him – that the "hen mal-lard" he made such an excellent passing shot on was in reality an eclipse drake. Here, the guideline, as it is for all hunting situations, stands – if in doubt, don't shoot.

Still the questions remains, how do you learn to tell one from the other? The best way for most hunters to learn duck identification is simply through practice and repetition. An afternoon spent at a nearby city park pond, or better yet, a national wildlife refuge armed with binoc-ulars and a good waterfowl identification book or pam-phlet (I recommend *Ducks at a Distance* published by the U.S. Fish and Wildlife Service; also on the Internet at

The drake mallard, probably the most popular and most easily recognized duck in North America.

Few birds can be mistaken for an adult drake (bull) pintail.

www.npwrc.usgs.gov/resource/tools/duckdist) is without question one of the best educational tools available. That, and plain, old-fashioned experience. Every time you see a flock of mallards, chances are you'll notice something new about the way they look, the way they act, and the way they respond to things like a decoy spread, calling, or even live birds on the water. Without you knowing it, all this information is recorded and catalogued, and is made available for what I'll term "recall" each and every time you see a flock of birds. Does it take a while to accumulate a library of waterfowl information? You bet it does, but it's some of the best and most enjoyable time you'll ever spend in the classroom.

All that said, let's now take a look at the various puddle, diver, and "other" duck species that waterfowlers in North America are most likely to see on any given day during the fall hunting season.

The puddle ducks

Mallard

a.k.a – Greenhead (drake); suzie (hen). The most common and one of the largest North American puddle ducks, and to many, *the* trophy bird among waterfowl. Found in all four major flyways. Very vocal. Hen has a loud quack; drake a lispy "dweek." Male sports a green head, white neck ring, brown chest, slate gray back. Hen a drab mottled brown. Both sexes with blue speculum edged in white.

Green-Winged Teal

Black Duck

a.k.a – Black mallard, black. Most common in the Atlantic and eastern Mississippi flyways. A large puddle duck, the drake black duck is a beautiful dusky color, with an iridescent blue speculum, orange legs, and yellow bill. Hens are similar, but slightly smaller and with an olive-green or gray mottled bill. Underwings of both sexes are a grayish-white or silver color – very apparent when the birds flush at close range or in bright sunlight. Hardy birds, blacks will often relocate to moving waters once local ponds, lakes, and marshes have frozen solid.

Pintail

a.k.a – Sprig, bull sprig (drakes). An incredibly regal duck, the drake's long neck and sharp, pointed tail provide good field markings. The drake is characterized by a brown head, white chest and neck, gray back, and buff rump patches (similar to the green-wing teal drake). Bill is black with pale blue sides. Hen sprig is brown overall, with an iridescent brown speculum bordered in white. Drakes can be longer than a mallard; however, not as heavy. Present in all flyways, but most abundant in the west and along the East Coast.

American Widgeon

a.k.a – Baldpate, robbers, poachers. Present in all four flyways; more so along the East and West coasts. The drake widgeon's blue bill tipped in black, white crown, mottled gray head, and white shoulder patch all

The American widgeon or baldpate, as he's sometimes called, is a familiar species in the Central and Pacific Flyways.

Our smallest North American puddle duck, the green-wing teal is as good on the table as he is quick on the wing.

help identify this sporty little duck. Hens are a brownish-rust overall, and share the black-tipped bill. Grazers, widgeons can often be found in damp pastures or on large, shallow pools of sheetwater where they feed on grasses and other plants. A second variety, the Eurasian or European widgeon, visits the coasts on occasion and can be told apart from his North American cousin by his cinnamon or rust-colored head, buff crown, and lack of his relative's green eye patch.

The Teals

a.k.a – Blue-wings; green-wings. Three subspecies in North America – the blue-wing, the green-wing, and the cinnamon. Blue- and green-winged teal are found in all four flyways; cinnamon teal are limited to the western United States. Small size, and swift twisting flight are characteristic of all three subspecies. Early migrants, blue-wing, so named for their pale blue shoulder patches, and cinnamon teal (overall coloration of drakes) will leave most northern climes by mid to late September. Green-wings will often stay north as long as they can find food and open water. Teal drakes "peep," while hens of all three subspecies have a quick, high-pitched quack.

Northern Shoveler

a.k.a – Spoonbill, spoony, grinning mallard, grinner, smiling mallard, Hollywood. Oversized bill (drakes, black; hens, light brown) best identifier. Drakes have green head, white chest and rump, black back, and yel-low eye. Hens very drab and mallard-like overall. Both sexes smaller than mallards. Most abundant in western (Central and Pacific) flyways, but found across country.

Gadwall

a.k.a – Gray duck, squarehead. Only North American puddle duck with a white speculum. Most abundant in Central Flyway, although found across the country in varying numbers. Drake a muted gray-black color overall with a black bill; hen a bit more brown, with bill edged in orange. Voice is a soft quack similar to a mallard's (hen), while the drake makes a sharper, shorter version.

Wood Ducks

a.k.a – Woodie, summer duck, squealer. No painter's palette has ever held all the colors found on the drake wood duck, nor ever will. So beautiful is the species, the bird's scientific name, *Aix sponsa*, means "betrothed." Present in all four flyways, the woodie is most abundant in the Mississippi Flyway, although my wife and I have at times seen excellent numbers in the Pacific Northwest. With his blood-red eye, multicolored bill, and kaleidoscope of blues, purples, golds, reds, blacks, and whites, the drake woodie is difficult to confuse with any other species, save the Mandarian – an uncommon import whose primary identifier is his upswept gold rump feathers, a gaudy element lacking on the wood duck. Hen woodies are drab birds, although not without their beau-

The American widgeon (background) is a beautiful bird…

…as is his European counterpart, the Eurasian widgeon. Note the similarities and the obvious difference.

The ringneck, pictured here, can be considered a cross-over, inhabiting both shallow-water ponds (puddles) and deep-water (diver) environments.

The only North American puddle duck with a white speculum (the lower edge of the wing), the gadwall or gray duck is easy to identify.

There is absolutely no mistaking the majesty and beauty that is the wood duck.

ty. Hens will have a white-ringed eye, speckled chest, and overall light olive coloration.

Ringneck

a.k.a – ringbill, blackjack. A handsome duck, the ringneck resembles the scaup with his black head and chest, and white sides and belly; however, the ringneck does, although somewhat difficult to see, sport his name-sake neck ring, as well as a black back—an easy-to-see difference between he and the scaup species. Characteristic, too, is his black-tipped bill with white touching ring and white facial border. Hens are mottled brown and gray, but share the black bill tip and white ring. Distributed in all four flyways, with heaviest numbers in the Mississippi Valley.

The Diving Ducks

Canvasbacks

a.k.a – Can. For decades this was, and still to many hunters is, the king of all waterfowl. A favorite among early American diners, the canvasback's high rating on the table made it a primary target for market hunters – a rating that unfortunately decreased populations almost to the point of extinction. Today, numbers have strength-ened to allow limited hunting opportunities. A large duck, the drake canvasback's white midsection, black chest and tail, and rusty red head and red eye all make for good field marks. A long, heavy, sloping bill and fore-head help set the can apart from his nearest counterpart, the redhead. Hens are light-bodied, with a brown-gray chest, neck, and head, and the characteristic sloping bill. Though found in all four flyways, the largest number of cans will be found either on the upper East Coast or, on the Upper Mississippi River.

Redhead

Similar in appearance to the canvasback with its namesake red head, black chest and tail, and white back and belly, the redhead lacks both the size and long chiseled profile of its more notable visual relation. In flight, the red-head can be distinguished from the can by its smaller size, faster wingbest, short bill, and puffy head. Hens, like most, are a drab brown mixed lightly with white. Both drakes and hens have a pale blue bill tipped in black.

Scaup

a.k.a – Bluebill, bills. Two subspecies, greater and less-er. Males are black fore and aft, with white midsection and trademark blue bill; hens have soft brown head and chest, white face patch, and light gray back and belly. Subspecies easily confused; however, greater has larger head and longer (white) stripe on the secondary feathers. Typically found on large bodies of water and in large groups known as rafts. Both subspecies found in all flyways, although most numerous in Mississippi and Atlantic.

Although primarily raised in captivity in the United States, the mandarin, pictured here on a pond in Washington state, occasionally goes wild, often sharing the company of the wood duck.

Goldeneye

a.k.a – Common goldeneye, whistler. Found in all four flyways. Drakes have an iridescent green head featuring a distinctive white "dot" at the base of the bill. Yellow (golden) eyes, black back, white chest and belly. Hens have a brown head, slate-gray back and underside, and a short, stubby bill tipped in brownish orange. Cavity nester; uses hollow trees like wood duck and hooded merganser. Loud, whistling flight. Barrow's Goldeneye drake similar, but with larger face patch and darker back. Found in Pacific and Atlantic flyways.

Bufflehead

a.k.a – Butterball. Comparable in size to the tiny green-wing teal (8 to 16 ounces), the drake bufflehead, with his black and white markings and puffy white crown, is a dapper little duck – though, unfortunately, not all that tasty on the table due to a diet high in animal matter such as insects, fish, and shellfish. Hen butterballs are smaller still, with white chests and a short white patch under each eye. While found in all four flyways, bufflehead are not commonly seen in hunters' daily bags, but rather taken as an incidental species.

The Other Ducks

Mergansers

a.k.a – Fish duck, sawbill. Three varieties include the red-breasted, common, and hooded (hoodie). The red-breasted sports brownish-red chest, off-white midsection and back, and green head with feathery crest; common is similar but lacks crest and chest markings. Hens are gray-white overall, with rusty head and crests. Both subspecies are large birds. Single file, low level flight, is the field mark. Hooded birds are smaller but more colorful. Drake has high, black head with distinctive white patch (hood), rust sides, white underbelly, and black back. Hen is a drab gray, but shares characteristic hatchet-shaped head. Hooded mergansers are more likely to frequent small woodland ponds and marshes; other subspecies found on fast, rocky rivers, and larger fresh and brackish waters.

Tree ducks

We first saw black-bellied whistling ducks while in southern Texas for a spring turkey hunt. Amazing birds with a high, melodic call, these ducks seemed as at home in the high branches as they did on the tiny potholes that dotted the ranch. To our surprise, we were told that the birds were excellent on the table. Drake and hen black-bellied ducks are similar in appearance, with the namesake black underbellies, brown chests and back, and light heads. Duck-like, the birds have exceptionally long legs and necks. Another whistling duck, the fulvous tree duck, is similar in size and shape; however, the overall coloration is a soft caramel brown, with striking bars on the back and

Drake common goldeneye

sides. Both races are much more common in Mexico and points south.

Eiders

A big duck often weighing 4 to 6 pounds, the sea-going Common Eider (King, Spectacled, and Stellar's eiders found in Alaska and the Arctic) frequents the Atlantic coast of the United States. Drakes are predominantly white above and black below, with a black mask or crown and large yellow-white bill. Hens, a mottled brown/black. Flight is strong, and typically low – often just above the surface of the water.

Scoters

a.k.a – Skunkheads, coots. Big, chunky sea ducks, scoters are found on both the East and West coasts. Three subspecies include the Common, White-winged, and Surf. Drakes black overall; however, white head patches (Surf) and eye patches (White-winged) help differentiate between races. Bills also serve as qualifiers, with the Common having a yellow bill, the White-winged black tipped in yellow/orange, and the Surf Scoter sporting a wild combination of white, yellow, red, and orange. Hens of all subspecies a charcoal brown.

Harlequin

The first and only harlequin ducks I've seen were a drake and hen on the East Fork of the Lewis River in Washington, one of the few states to feature this remark-

A hen lesser scaup, just one of five "new" species I harvested during my first year as a Washington resident.

Ruddy Duck

Redhead

able sea duck. And like the wood duck, photographs do the colorful drake harlequin little, if any, justice. Males sport a brilliant scheme of blues, rusts, blacks, and whites; while the hens are a buff brown above, white below. Not overly abundant anywhere, harlequins are found in the western and northern parts of the Pacific Flyway, and the extreme northeastern portions of the Atlantic, primarily off the New England coast. Secretive little ducks, harlequins are fond of fast-moving, rocky mountain streams, hence their nickname mountain duck.

Oldsquaw

Like the pintail, the ocean-going oldsquaw's long pointed tail provides a good field mark. Primary North American range includes the Great Lakes region and the Atlantic Coast, with lesser numbers in the Pacific Northwest. Drakes largely white with black chest, back, and chin patch; lighter in summer color phase. Hens show a white belly and darker back and wings. Often taken by hunters focusing on other species.

Ruddy

Widespread but not abundant. Primary range in the lower 48 states including the Pacific and Atlantic flyways. A small duck, often weighing less than 1½ pounds, the drake's upright, stiff tail, cinnamon body color, black crown, and white face patch are all excellent field marks. Bill is broad and pale blue. Hen ruddy is smaller than the drake, and is a light brownish-white overall.

2
Clothes and Accessories:
The Essentials

What do fishing lures, baseball hats, and .22 rimfire rifles have in common? Give up? Well, let me tell you that these three outwardly different things share one very interesting detail. It's virtually impossible – no, I'd say that it's definitely impossible, at least from a male standpoint – to have too many of any of them.

Such is the case concerning the garb and gear associated with the art of the waterfowler. From the very first moment the fledging – no pun intended – duck hunter steps into the marsh, he, and now, fortunately for our sake, or she begins a process of accumulation and collection the likes of which the world has seldom seen. A pair of hip boots here. A coat there. And another dozen assorted gloves and bags and hats certainly never hurt anyone. Besides, they don't take up much space, do they? Not in the 100,000 square foot storage sheds we waterfowlers call garages.

But is all this stuff necessary, these piles upon piles of neoprene and plastic? Of metal? And aluminum? Are the 13½ miles of decoy cord – Don't laugh. I currently have in my basement that very same distance of eight-pound monofilament fishing line. Why? You tell me – really necessary? Yes. And no.

Waterfowling is, in all honesty, a relatively equipment-intensive activity. Certainly, the amount of equipment differs depending upon the aspect of the activity. For instance, the fellow who walks into a local marsh intending on putting out his traditional half-dozen standard mallard blocks carries a reasonably light load, and he does so with a minimal amount of time spent in self-preparation. The big water layout shooter, on the other hand, might leave the house with an equipment list that reads something like a multi-million dollar Sam's Club shopping spree, not to mention looking like something out of a 1940s B-grade horror film. This gentleman's gear

The duck hunter's world is often a cold place, where ice and rain, snow and discomfort are frequent visitors to the blind.

may very well, and most likely will, consist of a tender boat and trailer, a layout boat, possibly two, with trailer, and a set of long-line decoys counted by the dozens. But wait! There's still a gun, dog, dip net, waders, camouflage jacket, blind bag, thermos, binoculars, chemical hand-warmers, lip balm, decoy bags, face paint, headnets, gloves, a second set of gloves for when the first set falls in the water, neoprene gloves, duck strap, duck calls, goose calls, an extra length of decoy cord, anchor, anchor line,

A good coat and a warm hat can make all the difference in the world, even under the most adverse conditions.

flashlight, headlight, nightlight….and on and on and on.

All that said, one question often comes to mind. Where does it all start? We've already established the fact that this process of hoarding and collecting is of the never-ending variety; still, the outfitting of the duck hunter, both novice and veteran alike, has to start somewhere. And with something. The answer? Clothes. Oh, yes, and a few accessories. But only a few.

Clothes, camo, and today's waterfowler

It's really somewhat difficult when writing on a national – hell, maybe even a global – level to discuss clothing and camouflage for the duck hunter. Waterfowlers in south Texas, for example, may never see a day below 40 degrees throughout the whole of the season. In Florida, it may be sunny and 60 all season. Out in the Pacific Northwest, it's going to rain. And it's going to rain for the vast majority of the 100 days that ducks are an option. Up north in Minnesota? Well, in a good year, those folks may very well spend the final two weeks of their duck season watching miniature icebergs float down the Mississippi. It's just like the real estate people say – location, location, location.

But despite this "clothes are a product of the environment" reality, there still remain some very basic rules of thumb when it comes to dressing for success in the field. That's not to say that sidetracks, a twist here and a new turn there, aren't permissible; in fact, a policy of improvise and adjust when it comes to clothing more often than not leads to the discovery of that magical combination of thermal and wool and cotton and synthetics that leads to consistent comfort. And a comfortable hunter, remember, is a much more successful hunter.

Clothes for the body

Seventy degrees or seven, it really doesn't matter. The secret to staying comfortable, hot or cold, in the field in terms of clothing is really no secret at all. In fact, it's only one word – layering. Layering allows you the option of putting on or taking off, depending upon the weather, a change in the weather, or other variables such as physical exertion.

Surprising to some, the process of layering is as important in warmer climates and conditions as it is in cooler temperatures. The clothing key, for lack of a better term, during periods of warmer weather is to dress so as to allow the inevitable perspiration that develops, often as a result of nothing more than existing, to wick away from the surface of the skin. Fortunately, today's hunters have at their disposal a long list of synthetic materials such as polypropylene, thinsulate, or any of a hundred different products with strange-sounding, weather-related names, all of which are designed with one thing in mind – to wick perspiration away from the body.

The duck hunter's hands – just one of the tools of the trade that need to be tended to.

Under colder conditions, these same synthetics work not only to wick perspiration away from the skin, but serve as a heat retention barrier. A first line of defense, so to speak. And so when the mercury falls, it's upon these initial foundations that additional clothing is layered.

For layering, few things beat wool. Wet or dry, this wonderful natural material retains body heat like no other. Good wool clothing, however, can be a bit on the spendy side. Fortunately, there are alternatives such as thermal, flannel, and fleece which, given today's advancements in material creation and manufacturing, can perform almost as well if not better than wool. And often for less than half the price.

Head, hands and feet

If a duck hunter is going to make a mistake in terms of clothing and dress practices, chances are it's going to involves one or more of the following appendages – the head, the hands, or the feet. What's even more important than this statement is the fact that regardless of how well you're layered between your ankles and your collar, if you're hands or feet are cold, you're cold. And that's all there is to that.

But for many people, these three problems areas, and the hands and feet in particular, prove the most difficult to keep warm and comfortable. And unfortunately the solution for one may not be the answer for the next;

however, what is a definite is that attention given these three problem areas can and in most cases will result in an overall increase in outdoor comfort.

Maybe it has something to do with the fact that heat rises. Regardless, it's a proven, scientific fact that the majority of a person's body heat is lost through the top of the head; that is, unless the top of the head is covered. And covered well. Under most cold weather conditions, the modern baseball cap just doesn't do the job. But watch caps, some complain, don't offer the shade like that of a billed ball cap. The answer? A billed watch cap. Or a reasonable facsimile thereof. During the 2000 Iowa waterfowl season, a time when temperatures regularly dipped into the single digits, I took to wearing what I called a Mad Bomber hat. Borrowed, meaning on indefinite loan, from a hunting partner, this flop-earred Browning product was soon discovered to be the warmest hat ever created. And I'm talking in the history of hats. And what was more, the bomber had the perfect bill – not too long and not too short. Heat loss via my scalp became a thing of the past, and I became a warmer, happier person.

Unlike some, I've never had much of a problem keeping my hands warm. I'm told that years of trapping bare-handed under frozen and semi-freezing conditions acclimated my hands to lower temperatures. True or not, I have discovered that as I get older, my hands tend to get a little colder during hunts in November and December. Because of this, I've started including two different sets of

Whether used for setting decoys or just keeping warm, neoprene gloves can provide the extra needed layer of protection against the elements. So, too, can a good cup of coffee.

gloves in my blind bag. The first, a full-fingered pair, are of the very common insulated jersey variety. My only alteration on these gloves was to remove the index finger on the right hand – my trigger finger – as I find it important personally to have skin-to-metal contact both when removing the safety and shooting. The second pair, and those that I wear when the temperature's aren't as extreme, is a fingerless rag wool set. Purchased for less than $10 from Wal-Mart, these fingerless wool gloves have been with me for several years now, and despite a couple tiny holes in the back of one, work extremely well, wet or dry.

For those with problem hands, the new chemical handwarmers can certainly be a godsend. Inexpensive, lightweight, and long-lasting, these tiny white packages of sawdust and metal shavings operate on the basis of a "quick-rust" process, a chemical reaction all too commonly seen but seldom thought of as a heat-producer. But it is, and fortunately so, as these little bags have more than once saved the hunt for waterfowlers from the Pacific to the Atlantic. One of the tricks that I use with good success during cold weather is to slip an activated hand-warmer into the back of each glove. Or in some cases onto the palm of my non-shooting hand. Protected from the wind as such, these handwarmers can be effective all day long. A second method for employing these items, and one which non-glove wearers such as myself find useful, is to put one or two into an insulated fleece muff

worn buckled around the waist. Not only does this practice keep hands warm, but eliminates any interference, psychological or otherwise, between gloves and gun.

Coats and wet-weather gear

As much as I hate to say it, size does make a difference when it comes to waterfowling coats. More precisely, the proper size makes a difference. Too often, I've watched as camo-clad renditions of the Michelin Man try to sit up or stand and shoot accurately at a passing flock of widgeon only to look like someone attempting hari-kari with a locust post. Trust me. It's traumatic to watch. Fortunately, and thanks to today's modern materials, bulk and the inability to put one's arms down to their side can be a thing of the past.

Inexpensive they're not, but good – and I mean high quality – waterfowl coats and parkas should last far beyond the life of the owner. What's more than just the durability and long life of these garments is the fact that most offer the wearer several different temperature-related options. A simple zip or two, and the coat's inner liner becomes a separate warm-weather coat. Reinstalled, and the parka will keep you as warm as would a camouflage sleeping bag. And on slow days in the blind, that might not be a good thing as it often leads to sleeping.

Too, most if not all of these waterfowl-specific parkas will serve double-duty as rain gear, thus eliminating the need for two separate coats and, fortunately for the pocket book, two separate expenditures. Again, the inner liner removed, and the outer coat, commonly called the shell, can be worn strictly as a rain garment. One of the nicest combination coats on the market today, and one which I've worn with good results from the Pacific Northwest to the Lake Erie breakwalls is the Quad Parka from Columbia Sportswear (**www.columbia.com**); however, there are several different makes and models available, including fine quality but much less expensive parkas offered by catalog distributors such as Cabela's and Bass Pro.

Camouflage

If you're interested at all in seeing verbal perpetual motion in action, just walk into your local sporting goods store and make the statement – "Brand X (your choice) camouflage is the BEST, and I'll tell you why." When you leave after having aged anywhere from one to 37 years, the conversation, or rather the argument, will still be raging on.

For all intents and purposes, it's next to impossible to accurately use the words "best" and "camouflage" in a sentence. Better than others, perhaps, but not best. The

A brown canvas coat like the one shown here remains one of the most traditional of waterfowling garments.

Get any three duck hunters together, and you're sure to see a variety of clothing and camouflage types and styles. Can you say 'fashion plates?'

Today's waterfowler has a wide range of camouflage garments from which to choose. Note the sling on this duck hunter's Remington, an indispensable item for the jump-shooter.

reason behind this inability to hold title to "The Best" is simple. Some patterns work, meaning they offer the finest in concealment, better than others depending entirely upon the situation and the location. That's it. Period.

For example, Realtree's Advantage Wetlands, a wonderful and very effective pattern that relies extensively on golds and tans and light browns, is tops for those hunting cattail marshes or cut corn fields in the Fall. That is, after the colors have changed. The same pattern during an early teal season, in a lay-out boat, or against a pin oak in the flooded timber, however, stands out like a turtle in a punch bowl. Likewise, Mossy Oak's Shadow Grass, an incredible pattern that must have been designed specifically with the Fall field hunter in mind. While this particular camouflage works well under some conditions, it too has its place.

A decision regarding choice of camouflage for the duck hunter, then, means choosing that pattern which offers the widest spectrum of effectiveness across the broadest band of situations and locations. What's all that mumbo-jumbo mean? Essentially, will the camouflage of choice be effective under 25 percent of your personal hunting conditions, or 75 percent? Is it good for two weeks in late September, or during the whole of October and November? True, today's deluge of camouflage manufacturers, patterns, and designs can make such a decision difficult. Maybe even confusing. Much more confusing, say, than 25 years ago when the choices ran the gamut from basic Woodland – you know, the old-fashioned dark green-light green-black-brown blobs – to, well, basic Woodland. Back then, buying camo was easy. Still, the choice is yours and yours alone.

Waders, hipboots, and other footwear

Unfortunately, some things never change. Take for instance the fact that today, as it was almost three decades ago, I find it physically impossible while wearing a pair of chest waders to get within 100 yards of a barbed wire fence – even a small section of old, rusted, forgotten, partially buried barbed wire – without there suddenly appearing great rends and rips in several assorted portions of my rubber apparel. Even in the Sahara and at the sight of such a strand of rusted wire, my waders would immediately begin to fill with water. And not just any water, but cold, make-things-shrink water. It's an art, I know, and one that I would be more than happy to pass along to future generations. To anyone.

Fortunately in today's waterfowling world, there are solutions to destructive problems such as mine, thanks in part to any one of several advances in duck hunting footwear. And while 100 percent bullet-proof chest waders may indeed be the stuff that duck hunters'

Hip boots, an inexpensive alternative to the more costly chest waders, and a good place to start with those new to the sport.

dreams are made of, the modern footwear of today comes as close to the ultimate in dryness and comfort as, well, a duck hunter is ever going to get.

But what about waders? Does today's waterfowler really need them in order to be successful? And if so, how does one choose from among the countless dozens of different makes, models, sizes, and configurations? Too, what about hipboots? Is there a place in today's waterfowling arena for these most introductory pieces of duck hunting paraphernalia? The answers are as many and as varied as are the camouflage patterns in your local sporting goods store; however, there are answers at least in part. The remainder, I'm afraid, can only be left up to personal preference. And perhaps the latest in outdoor fashion.

Our very first steps...in hipboots

Most duck hunters, myself certainly included, begin or began their waterfowling careers clad in a pair of ugly green rubber hipboots. Let me tell you why. First, if the boots weren't of the hand-me-down variety and therefore free, they were very inexpensive. That can be read 'cheap.' What sense was there, our fathers or grandfathers or uncles or whomever was teaching us the finer points of waterfowling said, in buying a pair of hipboots, or heaven forbid a pair of chest waders, that was just going to be outgrown in a year. Hell, some were out

Neoprene chest waders like this hunter wears here have grown in popularity over the past decade. Even the black lab has her own set.

grown even before the season ended. Secondly, and while times have changed to some extent today, when I was growing up in the early 70s, there were no chest waders made to fit the short, knobbly-kneed legs of a 10-year-old boy. And finally, there was the fact that regardless of whether we were encased in rubber from hip to toe as with hipboots, or head to toe with chest waders, the end result – wet – was still going to be the same. Looking back, I think the choice of hipboots was in part a safety measure as wet from the thighs down was a whole lot less severe and life-threatening than was damp from the neck down. Or at least that's what I was told.

Now with that nostalgic look back behind us, we're free again to discuss hipboots and their place, if one does exist, in the waterfowling world of today. It should come as no surprise to anyone that the key factor in the hipboot decision involves water depth; however, there are a handful of other considerations which should be given some thought when it comes time to choose between hip-high and chest-high. First, and most obviously, hipboots come from the factory with a 'hip-deep' water level limitation. That is unless the wearer doesn't mind, or in my case had years of getting accustomed to, getting wet to some degree. For the hunter gunning exclusively over shallow flooded fields from a pit or other type of permanent blind, or perhaps for the fellow who hunts only from a boat, hipboots might make an excellent choice. They're reasonably light, and most brands can come awful close to comfortable, even when they're worn for extended periods of time. Rolled down and fastened, hipboots can be substituted for a traditional pair of hunting or hiking boots; however, these hunting boots can pull double-duty should the levee break and the water rise. And finally, there may be some truth to the comment about hipboots and younger, impetuous hunters, those who might be inclined to take 'just one more step' or who just might not have the experience necessary to make a wise – and safe – wading decision. In this case, shorter boots might help keep a young charge within arm's reach and out of trouble.

But while hipboots can and do have their place, there's also a short list of downsides for prospective hip-high buyers to consider. Because of their short height, hipboots naturally do little to keep the wearer dry between hips and chest. And this can make all the difference in situations such as rain or snow, an off-balance fall, or, as happens quite frequently, where lying down suddenly in the mud outside the blind when your partner announces, "Get down. Here they come!" becomes a necessary thing. Finally, hipboots aren't nearly as inexpensive as they once were; in fact, a good pair of insulated rubber hipboots can cost as much or more than a more-than-adequate quality set of five-mil camouflage neoprene chest waders – boots that offer the wearer all the additional water depth, and then some.

Is there a bottom line in this discussion about hipboots? I'm afraid I have to answer this question by suggesting you ask yourself the question – Given (1) where I hunt and (2) how I prefer to hunt, are the limitations of hipboots really limitations? If not, stick with the hipboots; if so, read on.

The world of waders

I can still remember the Christmas I got my first pair of chest waders. Rubber Northerners, a Servus brand, they were. All wrapped up nice and neat and pretty by my Mother. And I can remember how my father, at that time the wizard of rubber pants – waders, that is – told me, "Now be careful with those. And don't rip 'em." He couldn't have cursed a man any more completely had he said to Nolan Ryan, "Hey. Do you know you're pitching a no-hitter?" Still, and while they were the first pair of chest waders I would mystically transform from boot to rubber sieve, they certainly wouldn't be the last. However, I digress.

Chest waders. Pros and cons.

1. **PRO** – You're not limited only to water hip-deep or shallower. This advantage opens up a much broader aquatic world to waterfowlers, allowing them to set decoys deeper, cross creek channels to get to out-of-the-way areas, stand comfortably and secure in flooded timber, and stay drier in all types of weather and field conditions.

2. **CON** – Chest waders should come with some type of simple warning that reads – "One more step? Don't try it!" For several reasons, high waders and high water don't necessarily go together. Those choosing chest waders should stay within their limitations, and should never forget that most elemental guideline – Use Common Sense.

3. **PRO** – Insulated chest waders, particularly those made of neoprene, can help keep you warm even under the most severe conditions. While hunting near Kramer, North Dakota several years ago, a place where the cold Canadian and Arctic winds are slowed only by wheat stubble, barbed wire, and the occasional fence post, we wore sets of 5-mil (five millimeter thickness; also comes in 3-mil for warmer weather) neoprene chest waders while field hunting simply to help keep us warm and ward off those terrible winds. Despite there not being any water within a mile or two of the morning's hunt, the snow geese and mallards didn't appear to mind.

Convertible waders like these from Rocky Shoes & Boots in Nelsonville, Ohio, are perfect for both early and late-season hunts.

4. **CON** – Chest waders can be uncomfortable. And at no time is this more true than during periods of cold weather when layers upon layers of clothing must be worn underneath. Fortunately, many of today's neoprene chest-highs such as the Teal from Rocky Shoes and Boots with its Ankle Fit feature have begun to emphasize comfort as much as durability, presumably after manufacturers finally came to the realization that some hunters will spend literally days in their waders.

5. **PRO** – Chest wader manufacturers offer hunters their choice of neoprene, cordura nylon, or traditional materials. As I mentioned earlier, neoprene, either 3-mil or 5-mil, is nice when the weather or the water is cold. In addition, neoprene is relatively easy to repair, often using nothing more than factory-supplied repair kits and a common household iron. While perhaps not as warm as neoprene, insulated cordura nylon waders are certainly no slouch when it comes to comfort. Not to mention that cordura is an excellent material choice for those hunters such as myself who cannot help but abuse a pair of chest-highs. Cordura is a a first-rate choice for timber hunters or those who frequently wade hazard-filled waters such as beaver swamps, rivers, or streams. Finally, there's rubber. Good old rubber. Still a decent all-around choice for the serious waterfowler; however, this age-old material has in recent years taken quite the backseat to both neoprene and cordura. Why? Even insulated, rubber has a tendency to get downright chilly. And it's not nearly as durable as the other two options, neither of which are susceptible to dry rot.

6. **PRO** – Modern chest-highs come in a wide variety of sizes, widths, and camouflage patterns. There are even chest waders – check either Cabela's or Bass Pro, ladies – designed specifically for women and children.

7. **CON (?)** – Chest waders are more expensive than hipboots; however, that does make perfectly good sense seeing as there's quite a bit more material goes into a pair of chest waders than into their smaller counterparts. Today, chest-highs can range in price from $50 for a low-end pair of uninsulated rubber boots to more than $250 for one of the new cutting-edge neoprene models, completely done up in the latest camouflage pattern. With chest waders, just like with many things, the old adage – You get what you pay for – certainly does hold true. Before buying, however, it's best to seriously consider (1) what you'll be using the waders for, and (2) how you'll be using them. In the long run, a good set of chest waders should last for several seasons, with each year just as warm and dry as the one before.

Zen and the art of wading

Luckily for many of us, the art of wading comes with few rules. Perhaps a better word, a term more precise than rule, would be postulates. Maybe absolutes. How about 'sure things?' These would include –

1. If you hurry, you will fall.

2. If you think about anything other than wading while wading, you will fall.

3. You will fall.

4. Anything dropped inside a pair of chest waders goes to that point farthest from your wrist and most difficult to reach.

5. The likelihood of a dropped object falling inside your waders while standing waist deep is in direct relation to the importance of that item. A paperclip or the last bite of ham sandwich? In the waders. The operating handle to your Remington 11-87? Outside the waders.

6. Likewise, the chance and location of a tear or rip is proportional to (a) the water depth, (b) the distance you are from warmth and a change of clothes, (c) the temperature, and (d) the possibility that you know where you hid the last remaining tube of repair glue.

7. Beavers can and often do dredge channels (a) overnight, (b) in front of your blind, and (c) miles away from any indication there might be beavers in the vicinity.

8. Did I mention you will fall?

Accessorizing

After all this talk of clothing and footwear, what else could the well-dressed and outfitted waterfowler possibly need in the way of gear? First, there's something with which to carry all the odds and ends, including but not limited to shells, calls, extra gloves, and so forth. And second, there are a couple items that while not necessities certainly make the waterfowling experience all the more enjoyable.

The blind bag – the duck hunter's catch-all.

Field bags, or blind bags as they're sometimes called, are to the duck hunter like cheek pouches are to a chipmunk – there's always room for one more thing, be it a kernel of corn, a hickory nut, or that second roll of duct tape. Still, they are very useful items, both for helping to keep the unorganized organized, and for getting the myriad things safely and securely into and out of the field. Not to mention, keeping them orderly and protected while in the field.

Currently, several different manufacturers make and market blind bags. Not surprisingly, they come in a wide range of sizes, styles, and – yes – camouflage patterns, many designed like fishing lures to catch the eye of the hunter first. Regardless of how attractive a bag might be, there are certain qualities that *your* bag should possess if it's going to serve its purpose and serve it well. One of the most important of these qualities is durability. Waterfowlers, myself included, are notorious for, how shall I say it, abusing their hunting gear. In our defense, now, a large part of this stems from the conditions, climactic, environmental, and otherwise, under which we use this equipment. Still, there are seldom times when I don't finish a trip without at least a portion of my gear either being wet, muddy, frozen, scratched, or all of the above. This said, it's vital that anything carried into the field, bags included, should be of the highest quality your wallet can manage. On a final quality-related note – Be sure to check, test, and double-check such high-stress points like handles, shoulder straps, zippers, and hook-and-loop attachments before deciding on a blind bag. Typically, these will be the bag's weakest points, and here the old adage of something being only as strong as it's weakest point most certainly holds true. Oh, and make sure the bag is indeed waterproof as it should be, particularly on and around the bottom and the bottom seams. Few things are as aggravating as is digging through a bag that has been stored in the bottom of the boat or blind, only to find that everything in the bottom is waterlogged. The bottom line here is that while good blind bags aren't going to be cheap, *bad* blind bags are.

Size is another consideration when it comes to deciding on a blind bag. Ideally, the bag should be big enough to carry the gear necessary for the most extensive or equipment intensive outing you might enjoy, yet not so big as to (1) be bulky or awkward to carry or otherwise transport, or (2) provide the opportunity to pack 100 pounds of gear when two would suffice. Something that I do consider when shopping for a blind bag is the fact that I will often use the bag as a headrest, particularly when hunting fields or when sprawled prone in a layout boat such as our Aqua-Pods. Because of this, I'm always looking for a bag that's well padded, especially on top, as well as of the proper size – square – and height – 10-12 inches – so that it can pull double-duty as a pillow.

Duck hunters don't have to be cold, thanks to lightweight portable heaters like this small propane unit by Coleman.

The contents of my blind bag will vary depending upon the type of hunting being done as well as other variables such as the duration of the trip, location, and even the time of year. Early in the season, for instance, my bag will always contain a small spray bottle of insect repellent, an item seldom necessary during mid-November diver hunts on the Mississippi. There are, however, some what I'll call "stock" items that can be found in my blind bag regardless of the calendar page. Being of the Type A personality, these items are checked and go into the bag the night before the hunt, making this process just one less thing that I have to concern myself with before heading afield. For most hunts, my bag will include –

Two duck calls	Two goose calls
1 box shotshells	Two pair of gloves
Camouflage face paint	Face paint remover pads
Duck strap or tote	Headnet
½ roll decoy cord	Bushnell compact binoculars
Gerber multi-tool	8-10 Tungsten BBs
Energy bars	Flexible water canteen
Toilet paper (Always!)	Chemical handwarmers
Extra batteries for Robo-Duck (optional)	

Although appearing like quite the lengthy list, these items are for the most part small and lightweight, and all can be carried in a medium-sized bag. Quite often, I'll

In some situations, all-terrain vehicles can be used instead of strong backs as beasts of burden.

include my Nikon N60 camera and a half dozen rolls of slide film, all enclosed in their own waterproof bag within the bag. Even with this, all my gear easily fits in a bag – I'm using the All Seasons bag by Final Approach (541-476-7562, or ***www.finalapproachblinds.com***) – that measures only 12 by 12 by 12, *and* works wonderfully as a pillow.

The last item I'll include in my blind bag is a collection of things that I refer to as a catch-all. Over the years, I noted those things that I've always needed and never seemed to have, and finally put them all together in one Zip-locked, waterproof bag. This bag includes –

Tin of aspirin	Antacids
Bandaids	Roll of electrical tape
Safety pins, various sizes	½ dozen toothpicks
Visine (eye wash)	Roll of dental floss
Cheap tweezers	

All told, the gear in a blind bag organized as such will allow most hunters to spend all day in the field comfortably.

And finally, the two things that I personally won't go afield without. Perhaps it's because I'm getting older and wiser, though most would disagree with the latter, instead voting strongly in favor of the former. Either way, I have learned that there really are no substitutes for ankle gaiters and floating gun cases.

Ankle gaiters, for those still enjoying the thrill of

pants that ride up to mid-thigh underneath chest waders or hip boots, are nothing more than strips of neoprene that are wrapped tightly around the bottoms of the pants and secured in most cases with a hook-and-loop fastener. Their purpose is simple, that being to keep the cuffs where they belong – around your ankles. Certainly, today's store-bought ankle gaiters are a bit more expensive than the round or two of duct tape we grew up using; however, these little wonders can be worn more than once, will pay for themselves several times over by season's end, and, for the fashion conscious, look a hell of a lot better than tape.

Today, I very seldom go into the field without a floating gun case. Whether hunting from a boat in open water, standing in a shoreline blind, or lying flat on my back in a stubble field, a good gun case helps protect my shotgun before, after, and during the hunt. Many of the cases currently available come in a variety of camouflage patterns, and offer such in-the-field conveniences as shoulder straps, and choke tube and shotshell pouches. But perhaps the biggest advantage to getting into the habit of carrying your shotgun into the field in a case is that word "floating." It only takes one watery save, or one muzzle that *didn't* get plugged with mud and dirt to more than pay for the cost and, if there indeed is any, the inconvenience of one-more-thing carried into the marsh.

No place to sit in the marsh? This hunter solved that problem with a light, easily carried camouflage ladder. Price? One dollar at a garage sale.

Small boats too, like the AquaPod pictured here, can help get gear into and out of the field quickly and easily.

What makes a waterfowl gun? Ask the hunters who own (left to right) a Beretta 390, Benelli Super Black Eagle, Benelli Nova, Remington 11-87, or Mossberg 500. I'm sure they'll be happy to tell you. Note the Jones Adjustable Buttplate on the Beretta 390.

3

Taking up Arms

In the days before steel shot, I carried into the marsh my father's first gun, a Winchester Model 24 double, 16-gauge nonetheless, complete with double triggers and a tendency to fire both barrels simultaneously whenever I wore gloves. Since the advent of and mandatory requirement for non-toxic ammunition, the Winchester has been retired from waterfowling. Pheasants, occasionally, and the odd fox squirrel or two, but no steel.

Since the retirement of the Model 24, I've gone through a procession of various duck guns. A 16-gauge Remington Model 1100, a Mossberg 500 pump, a Browning A-5 Sweet Sixteen – I think I personally kept the 16-gauge alive during the late 1970s and early 80s. And most recently, a Remington Model 11-87. Purchased in 1988, the 11-87 has seen duty in a dozen different states and has reliably cycled what I could only guess would be tens of thousands of rounds of ammunition – big, small, and everything in between. Today, the Remington's my gun of choice when I head into the field or the marsh. But is it the *perfect* waterfowl gun? For me based solely on performance and results over the past 12 years, it's as close as I'm ever going to get; however, for most duck hunters, there's no better way to start an argument than with the simple statement, "This gun's the best, and I'll tell you why."

The waterfowl gun

Although I wouldn't expect any two duck hunters to agree completely on what constitutes THE ultimate waterfowl shotgun, I think I would be safe in saying that all would agree that there are several characteristics that such an ultimate gun would possess, regardless of the make, model, or price point.

The duck hunter's fowling piece. No job to big. No obstacle insurmountable.

Today's duck gun must be able to operate under even the most extreme conditions. Ice? No problem for this Remington 11-87, unless you're a pintail.

Even muddy, this hunter's Mossberg functioned flawlessly.

1. **Durable and rugged** – In more cases than not, duck hunting is not for the man or woman who doesn't like to get dirty. Mud, dirt, dust, sand, snow, water, weeds, dog hair – it's just all part of the duck hunting scene. Sure, we can try to keep both our gear and ourselves as clean and dirt-free as possible; however, such attempts are often an exercise in futility. That's why, plain and simple, the waterfowler's firearm needs to be both durable and rugged. This shotgun can and will operate under a wide range of weather and environmental conditions. And while we will try to prevent them, scratches, dings, and dents are inevitable; still, this particular firearm should stand up well, or even better than well, to what many, myself included, could only call abuse. But it's kind abuse.

2. **Dependable** – Nothing is quicker to frustrate than something that should work and doesn't. Hence, the duck hunter's shotgun needs to be dependable. Yes, there are times when the gun gremlins will invade the closet and create havoc among small yet very vital parts such as O-rings and operating handles. And, yes, dependability does rely in large part on an observance of routine and thorough maintenance. Still, the rules here are relatively simple. Keep it clean, keep it well-fed, and it will reward you with dependability.

3. **Simple in design and function** – It doesn't matter if we're talking about shotguns or space shuttles, the fact remains that simple is always better. This probably explains why so many waterfowlers opt for pump-action shotguns rather than the fancy, newfangled autoloaders. And there's probably quite a bit of truth in these decisions; however, thanks to advancements in design, today's modern autoloaders are in many cases as elemental from a parts and operation standpoint as are the pump guns of old. Simple in design and function, too, translates into easy to clean and maintain, which in turn takes us back to Rule Number 2, dependability.

4. **Comfortable** – By comfort, I mean simply that a shotgun's of little or no use *if* you don't shoot it well. Esthetics are nice, certainly, but I've been witness to some tremendous displays of shooting by hunters wielding some of the ugliest shotguns on the face of the planet. Tape, paint, scratches, dents. It didn't seem to matter, least of all to the ducks. The bottom line is, then, that it doesn't matter what the piece looks like. What matters is how well you shoot it.

Does size matter: A gauge discussion

Let's face facts. In a discussion on duck hunting and gauge selection, there's really only two serious conversationalists left at the table. Those that shoot the 10-

Age has nothing to do with it. Purchased in the early 1970s, this Remington Model 1100 still has its original O-ring – that after lit-erally tens of thousands of rounds.

With an improved choke tube, this Remington 11-87 served this hunter well under the close-quarter shooting conditions of a woodland pothole.

The pump has been for decades a favorite among waterfowlers. Why? It keeps going and going and going.

gauge, and those that carry a 12. All right. In all fairness, let me say that every now and then, the 20-gauge makes his presence known. Still, and but for a handful of 20-gauge exceptions, it's a party of two.

Now that I've managed to greatly irritate fans of the smaller bores, let's take a look at some thoughts and theories that might help explain just why the list has gotten so short.

The 10-gauge

In the days before non-toxic shot, only the diehard goose hunters had 10-gauges. Oh, I'd see one every now and then in the duck marsh, a double barrel usually. Most toted by masochistic individuals either with shoulders wide as a barn door or misconceptions about shotgunning physics the size of a small New England state.

Once non-toxic shot became mandatory nationwide in 1991, however, many duck hunters across the country began to give the 10 some serious thought. Their thinking was that to be effective with this new lighter and less energy-retentive ammunition, their shotshells would have to provide a greater number of hits on-target. And in order to do this, these same shotshells would then have to contain more pellets. More pellets – more hits. Or, lacking more pellets, then perhaps bigger, more energy-retentive pellets. Either way, the answer, or so it was thought, was to go up in shotshell hull size, thus increasing shot charge or payload.

Enter the 10-gauge. Within months of the mandatory non-toxic requirement going into effect in '91, the phrase – "I gotta get me a 10" – was shouted, whispered, and mumbled in duck blinds from coast to coast. However, the fervor was short-lived, due in large part to the many rapid and continuing improvements and advancements in non-toxic ammunition, as well as to the increasing availability of ballistics research and testing information concerning these new shotshells. And more significantly, their effectiveness or lack thereof through a wide range of variables, the most impressive of which has involved pellet size and energy comparisons.

So when the dust finally settled following the Fall of '91, it was primarily the goose hunters who had kept the big-bore 10-gauge alive. And in many cases, justifiably so. Big birds, geese often require substantial charges of exceptionally large pellets, pellets sometimes quite a bit larger than would typically be used for ducks. With today's improved non-toxic ammunition, these ball bearing-sized projectiles simply aren't necessary for the duck hunter, even with a target the size of an adult mallard. That said, the question remains – Does the 10-gauge have a place in the modern duck hunter's arsenal? Probably not out of necessity. But will they always be found in the duck blind? Without question.

In the right hands and under a watchful eye, the light 20-gauge can be an adequate duck gun; however, it does have its limitations.

Few 16 gauges like the Remington 1100 this young Washington waterfowler is using are seen in the field today. A shame, as they continue to be a more-than-suitable alternative to either 12s or 20s.

The 12-gauge

I'm going to go out on a limb and refer to the 12-gauge as the duck hunter's workhorse. Without precise statistical data, I'd still feel very safe in saying that nine out of every 10 waterfowlers – and I'm talking duck hunters here – head into the field with a 12-gauge in tow. Yes, that particular shotgun may chamber only 2¾-inch shotshells. Or it may be something like Mossberg's Model 835 Ulti-Mag or Remington's Model 11-87 Special Purpose Magnum, guns capable of handling anything from the lightest 2¾-inch steel trap loads to the biggest stick of dynamite 3½-inch shotshells on the market today. Regardless of the configuration, it's the 12 that wins the title of Most Commonly Seen Shotgun in the modern marsh.

Now, I'm going to take this one step further, and say that of these nine 12-gauges, eight, if not all nine, will be chambered to accept the popular 3-inch shotshell. In fact, I can only recall meeting one individual over the course of the past decade who carried, always and without fail, a 12-gauge that could be fed *only* 2¾-inch shotshells – my Father. For years, I tried to explain the many positives associated with the larger 3-inch shotshells, things such as payload, pattern density, and the ability to increase shot size without jeopardizing performance. But alas, all was in vain. His response? "I can kill any game bird in North America with this gun, and then some," he'd say. And the worst part was he'd done it several times over. Needless to say, it's difficult if not impossible to convince a Czech with proof otherwise. However, I digress.

As should now be obvious, there are three choices when it comes to the modern 12-gauge: the 2¾ inch, the 3-inch, and the 3½ inch. Speaking in the most basic of terms, the difference between the three is purely payload; in other words, hull capacity. For example, there are approximately 150 pellets contained in one ounce of steel #3 shot. Given that figure, we see –

12-gauge	Max shot charge	Pellet count
2¾ inch	1¼ oz.	187
3 inch	1⅜ oz.	208
3½ inch	1%₆ oz.	234

But does an average 23.5 pellet difference between the various hull sizes present something significant in the field? In the short term, meaning perhaps over the course of a single hunting season, probably not; however, in the long run, that being the case where hundreds upon hundreds of rounds are expended – then, yes, these 23.5 pellets can add up to something that most would find substantial. Too, you can look at the difference this way. If a clean harvest requires from four to six pellet hits, both in vital areas and with sufficient retained energy, then these 23.5 additional pellets have in theory given you four to six more chances to bring your bird down.

The task, then, becomes putting these four to six additional pellets, or another collection of four to six pellets, in the right place at the right time. Personal shooting styles and abilities aside, some shotguns will perform more effectively when fed 3-inch shotshells, while others, perhaps of an identical make and model, will pattern much better using either 2¾- or 3½- inch ammunition. These differences between individual shotguns and their performance with various types of ammunition are best discovered on the range in front of a patterning board – a topic which will be discussed shortly.

In the end, it becomes clear that the case of 2¾- inch 12 versus the 3-inch versus the 3½- inch is one based on a combination of personal preference and the understanding and acceptance of limitations; however, even a 155mm howitzer has its limitations. Results and performance, then, are dependent upon the man or woman either punching the primer or tugging the cord.

The 20-gauge

I don't believe I'm wrong in saying that steel shot has done to the 20-gauge exactly what the 3-inch 20 did to the 16-gauge so many years ago. It's made it, for all intents and purposes, obsolete. With its 1%₆ ounce magnum payload, or 159 #3 steel pellets, the 20-gauge as a consistent, effective – key words – duck gun is meant for the disciplined shooter who can recognize and adhere to the bore's 30- or perhaps 35-yard limitations. Mallards or widgeon over the decoys? Yes. Wood ducks at close quarters at a hole along a timbered creek? Yes. At ranges in excess of 35 yards, or with shotshells containing pellets larger than #2 steel (125 pellets per ounce)? Probably not.

Quickly, let me say that these words hurt me as much as they might many of the parents out there who with good intentions had planned on getting Billy or Joey or Jenny a lightweight, practically recoil-free 20-gauge pump gun or autoloader so that he or she might join the gang during the upcoming duck season. The thing is, though, that despite the factual evidence, the 20-gauge can still play a role as a youngster's first duck gun; however, that gun must also come complete with the aforementioned limitations, limitations which must be explained, practiced, and enforced by the child's instructor.

The 16, 28, and .410

In most locales, the sight of either a 16- or 28-gauge, or heaven forbid, a .410 in the duck marsh is cause sufficient to contact the local newspaper and ask that they send out both a reporter *and* a photographer. Truth is, you very, very seldom see any of these guns being used in the role of a waterfowl piece any longer. And the reason is simple – non-toxic shot. Originally, the reason had to do with a complete lack of ammunition for these particular bores and caliber – a financial thing really as shotshell manufacturers, struggling to get a grip on this newly introduced federal mandate, simply could not justify the cost involved with the production of a full and traditional complement of shotgun fodder. Duck hunters shot 10s and 12s, and therefore the manufacturers made 10-gauge and 12-gauge non-toxic ammunition. Oh, there were some 20s out there being used, but they were certainly in the minority. Essentially, it was a clear cut case of supply and demand. For the 16, the 28, and the .410, there was no demand; therefore, there was no supply.

Today, non-toxic alternatives for the 16- and 28-gauge, as well as the .410 are indeed available. Fans of the 16 may choose to shoot steel or bismuth; those shooting either the 28 or .410 are for the moment limited to bismuth. But shotshell availability does not a waterfowl gun make. With shot charges ranging from 1⅛ ounce in the 16 to an unimpressive 9⁄16 ounce in the .410, these particular-gauges and calibers can easily make even the finest shooter feel somewhat undergunned when it comes to consistently and cleanly harvesting waterfowl. And justifiably so, particularly in the case of the .410. Like the 20-gauge, both the 16 and perhaps the 28 can, in very skilled and disciplined hands, be considered ade-

Ever the perfectionist, shotgunning writer Phil Bourjaily marks another pattern target. The successful duck hunter knows that range time is as valuable or more so than field time.

quate choices for short-range field experiences such as the aforementioned mallards over decoys or close-in wood ducks along the timbered stream. Once, however, shot sizes in these particular gauges increase so as to potentially allow clean harvests at longer ranges, pattern density and therefore performance begins to suffer. For some, it's a sad fact, this non-toxic demise of these traditional small bores. Sad, but nonetheless true in most instances for today's waterfowler.

Ammunition

The case of duck hunting and ammunition selection is a little more clear cut, just a little more definite than is the quest for the ultimate waterfowl shotgun. Steel #6s, for example, are futile at 65 yards, while steel BBs are a bit on the large size for 25-yard widgeon hovering over the decoys. Each has its place, and each is similarly out of place in various situations. Fortunately, for those still uncertain as to the lead to non-toxic conversion tables, the decision as to which alternative shotshell load to use is relatively easy, thanks to that already familiar lead rule – match the load to the thing and the place. Centerfire rifle, muzzleloader, archery equipment, shotgun. The piece in question matters not. What does matter is knowing what constitutes what some call "too much gun," and knowing what isn't enough.

In this book, I'm not going to get into an in-depth

Although steel shot, due to its lower price, is the most popular non-toxic alternative to lead, bismuth and other metals are fast catching on.

discussion on shotshell ballistics. Nor am I going to talk about the different non-toxic alternatives to lead as they rate on the Diamond Hardness scale. What I want to provide is, first, just a tiny bit of techno-explanation about shotgun pellets and shotshells in general, and secondly, a very basic set of guidelines that will assist you as you make these shotshell decisions.

Steel is not lead. Lead is not steel.

Years ago while standing at the edge of a local marsh with my father on the eve of Opening Day, we happened onto another father-son team who, as we discovered shortly, we would be sharing the marsh with the next morning. As was the case during the early 1990s and the introduction of the non-toxic requirement, the conversation eventually turned round to the evil that was steel shot.

"I don't like this steel shot at all," said the father portion of the duo. "Yep, the days of 100-yards shots are over and done with. Not going to do that with this new steel stuff."

A short distance and some time later, I questioned my father concerning the man's statement. "I didn't know that the 100-yard days were ever here," I said. His Czechoslovakian eye-roll, a now-patented expression I'm sure, was all I needed.

Like many waterfowlers in the opening days of the 90s, this gentleman was having a difficult time accepting the fact that he could no longer take his favorite 1½ ounce load of lead #5 shot into the duck marsh. At least

not legally. Still, it's something that we as waterfowlers all had to adjust to; that is, if we wanted to continue hunting ducks and geese.

And while acceptance of this new mandate was difficult, learning to live with and shoot these non-toxic alternatives proved for many an even more frustrating undertaking. Why? Simple – steel is not lead. That's the bottom line. Once you leave behind the fact that this steel, like lead, is a collection of small spherical objects contained in a plastic case or hull, most if not all of the similarities between the two substances comes to an immediate halt. What, then, are the differences? Although there are several, one in particular stands far above the rest.

Lead is heavy; steel is light. To address this issue, let's first look at a simple but very important mathematical equation. Weight and mass, along with velocity, contribute directly to energy. In other words, an object's weight and size, combined with its speed, directly translates into the force this object has on another object. Because steel is lighter than lead, a #6 steel pellet does not have the same energy or force that a #6 lead pellet does under identical firing situations and circumstances. How do you achieve equality then? It's simple. You just increase the size of the steel pellet until the ratio balances. In most cases, the pellet size increase rule has been two pellet sizes. If, for instance, you favor #5 lead loads, the comparable steel equivalent would be #3. So far, this theory has worked relatively well in the field; however, there are – surprise! – other things to be considered.

Shock is just one of these "other" things. Soft, heavy, and easily deformed, lead pellets produced an incredible amount of shock on-target. If you'll remember, it's shock and hits in vital areas that result in clean and consistent harvests. Unfortunately, steel pellets, because of their hardness, are not prone to this deformation and therefore, at comparable lead velocities, did not produce an equal shock value. Something had to be done. And something was.

Recently, the makers of steel shot have attempted to address another of the energy transfer variables, speed, as well as this shock issue by introducing lines of high-velocity steel ammunition. Here, the thought is that an increase in pellet size (mass) *and* velocity (speed) would produce a result that might even more closely resemble the performance provided by the now-defunct lead loads in terms of shock and energy retention. In some cases, speeds increased dramatically – 1265 feet-per-second (fps) in the Winchester Super-X 12-gauge 3-inch 1⅛ ounce load to 1450 fps in the Supreme High Velocity Super Steel load in an identical gauge, chamber, and shot charge. Initially, results with these new loads were less than desired; however, researchers and engineers for Winchester and other manufacturers have since

Non-toxic ammunition has come a long, long way since the early days of steel shot, as evidenced by this wide selection which includes tungsten, tungsten mixes, bismuth, and high-velocity steel.

tweaked and tested and tried a long list of combinations until today, high-velocity steel shotshells are an excellent, and what's more, an effective alternative to some of the present more costly options.

As hinted at with 'more costly options,' steel shotshells are not the only game in town for the duck hunter. Currently, fowlers can choose from a variety of non-toxic alternatives including bismuth, tungsten, tungsten-polymer, and most recently, Hevi-Shot, a lead-free material that more closely resembles lead in elemental characteristics and performance than do any of the present alternatives. And this, "I act like lead, but I'm not lead" concept, is the true Holy Grail of the whole of the non-toxic shotshell industry. True, some of these substances, Hevi-Shot for instance, certainly do appear and perform lead-like; however, the downside is the cost. Here, differences between steel and non-lead/non-steel can be dramatic if not intimidating, and many range from as low as .35¢ - .50¢ per shotshell with steel to $1.75 or more per round with one of the other choices. In time, it's hoped by many that the price of these non-steel shotshells will fall to the point as to make them affordable to the general duck hunting population; however, until such a time as that happens, waterfowlers from coast to coast will make do, and make do well, with the modern steel offerings which are – thankfully – a vast improvement over those we first started with in the early 1990s.

Shot size: A brief discussion

As was mentioned earlier, shot size with non-toxic plays as important a role in consistency and success as it did in the pre-steel lead days. Matching the shot size to the game being hunted, just like coordinating rifle caliber and big game animal, is not without its exceptions and special cases; however, the following chart does provide a more-than-reasonable set of guidelines for those questioning where to begin the selection process.

In this chart, only shot size is discussed. Not shot charge (weight), pellet count, or gauge. Again, these are only recommendations. Patterning, range time, practice, and in-the-field performance will be the ultimate decision-maker.

Steel Shot size	Application/comments
#6	Small ducks at close range; good swatter (cripple) load
#4	Small ducks; early season birds; marginal over-decoy load
#3	Early season, all ducks; over-decoy load; comparable to lead #5 (maybe)
#2	Good all-round choice; comparable to lead #4; good pattern density
#1	Larger ducks; late-season birds; sea/diver ducks; pass-shooting
#BB	Pass-shooting; sea/diver ducks; late-season

Choke choice for today's duck hunter is a matter of tested performance. This means time spent on the range.

Choke: A similarly brief discussion

In the initial hub-bub that was the introduction of non-toxic shot, the subject of choke certainly wasn't forgotten. Nor was the matter of which choke to use with what shotshell and in what application any longer a simple or traditional – long shots, full choke; close-range, open choke – type of decision.

No, steel shot changed everything the waterfowler had learned about choke selection and pattern performance. Or so it was thought. Originally, the guidelines in terms of choke-steel combinations was one of opposites. "Open is better," said many supposedly in the know. "And you don't need a full choke," they continued. Under these new mandates, modified choke users such as myself were advised to look strongly at improved cylinder constrictions; full chokers, on the other hand, were to (1) throw their full choke tubes away, or, lacking interchangeable chokes, (2) have the last two inches of their favorite scattergun carved away and replaced. Drastic measures to be sure.

The reasoning was this. Due to steel's hardness, these new pellets, when fired, didn't flow as smoothly down the barrel and compress as uniformly when passing through the choke. In short, they reacted less politely to being squeezed in those last two inches prior to freedom. This reaction was even more apparent with the larger size pellets, which liked the thought of being constricted even less than did their smaller cousins. Too, these new steel shotshells did indeed pattern a bit tighter than their toxic predecessors. Again, the hardness of the material played a role; however, so too did the newly-designed wads used in these shotshells – thicker, heavier wads and shot cups, all designed to, in a traditional sense, hold patterns together, and yet in a less-than-traditional way, protect soft steel shotgun barrels from damage due to contact with the much harder steel used to make the pellets.

But, like all things non-toxic, this original way of thinking about chokes and choke selection began to change. At least where the smaller shot sizes were concerned. Research, defined as hundreds of thousands of rounds fired, patterned, analyzed, and evaluated, began to show that with steel shot sizes from #2 to #7, modified chokes were still modified chokes, improved were improved, and – surprise – full were full. Debunked now was the myth that the full choke tubes or full-choked barrels were to be thrown out; however, these new developments did place a renewed emphasis on the importance of individual patterning and testing. In other words, it again became necessary for the shooter – you – to spend time on the range shooting a variety of shotshell, shot size, and choke combinations in order to find that – recipe is what I call it – which works best in your particular firearm.

Unfortunately, the larger steel shot sizes - #1 through #BBB, #T, and #F – still resisted being pushed through a full choke. And the truth is, they probably always will, simply because of their size. Think of it as pouring first a cup of sand and then a cup of marbles through the same funnel. The sand flows freely from top to bottom, while time after time, the marbles require some poking and prodding to get them through – if they'll go through more than one at a time at all. This reluctance to move smoothly from chamber to muzzle results in erratic or blown patterns; that is, patterns that aren't consistent, and often contain oddly shaped or located holes – holes that can be big enough to allow even a bird the size of an adult mallard to pass through unscathed, particularly at longer ranges. Hence, the decision has for the most part been one of a modified choke in those situations which call for the larger steel shot sizes.

Is it or isn't it? Range estimation

Unfortunately, there is no cut-and-dried, 100 percent, all-the-time answer or guide to the question of whether or not a duck is in range; that is, close enough to be killed and killed quickly. Weather conditions, variations in species size, lighting, shotgun choice, ammunition, shooting ability, even how well an individual sees. All are variables that combine to make range estimation with flying targets one of the most difficult tasks faced by the waterfowler.

What makes this task particularly frustrating is the fact that in 99 out of 100 situations, the medium that surrounds the duck or ducks – the sky – provides nothing in the way of distance reference marks. In other words, there's nothing in the sky next to, beyond, or in front of the target bird that the bird can be compared to in order to make a decision as to distance. Think of it this way. Place a Harley-Davidson motorcycle, a Volkswagen, and a Ford pickup at different points on a football field. Now, stand at one of the goal lines, and write down the distance between your goal line and each of the machines. It's relatively easy to guess how far away each is, mainly because you have a wealth of things to compare each to. The other goal post, the other machines, the sidelines, the seats, the yardage markers, and so on. Now, hang that same Harley in space against the clear blue sky and see if it isn't a little harder to guess. Such is duck hunting.

Fortunately, there are some techniques that you can use to make estimating range a little bit less stressful. Not to mention, a lot more productive from a harvest standpoint. The first of these is nothing more than plain, old-fashioned experience learned by repetition. It's the same method used by those avid duck hunters who can quickly glance at a twisting, turning knot of black and grey, pre-dawn silhouettes and matter-of-factly say "teal" or "widgeon" or whatever. They've seen it enough, they've heard it enough, and they've proved themselves right or wrong enough times to know what is what. This ability, however, does take time and the aforementioned repetition. Once acquired, though, it can be one of the most reliable methods by which to judge distance. Not infallible but very reliable nonetheless.

Size is another way of determining distance. A drake mallard flying by at 60 yards, for instance, will appear smaller than the same bird at 30 yards. Here again, repetition can often be the best instructor when using this method. Some shooters I know have taken this technique a step further, and will actually use a laser rangefinder to "shoot" birds during the off-season. This technique provides both an accurate measurement of distance, as well as a visual comparison that they can then use later under field conditions. Other hunters, lacking high-tech gadgetry like laser rangefinders, will simply hang a harvested mallard at various known distances and practice as such.

A third method relies on color, visual clarity, or a combination of the two. Some hunters will say that when a bird's eye, bill, or feet can be seen clearly and accurately, that bird is within reasonable shooting range. Others

What does 30 yards look like? Forty yards? Improvement means knowing.

will claim that once certain colors or patches of color, such as a drake mallard's neck ring or a drake widgeon's white head patch, can be seen in sharp detail, then that bird is in range. Reliable? To some extent, yes; however, the conditions typically have to be reasonably moderate, where moderate here means sunny or at the very least relatively clear, in order for this particular method of range estimation to be accurate. Fog, for instance, has a way of distorting things such as size, shape, speed, and above all, color, thereby making all three of these range estimation tools practically null and void. In these instances, hunters will find themselves reverting to good, old-fashioned experience. That, and a rule of thumb which I have tried to live by throughout the whole of my duck hunting career – "If for an instant you question yourself as to whether or not a bird's in effective shooting range, it's probably not." If in doubt, wait.

Those hunting over decoys have a fourth technique that they can use to facilitate range estimation. When setting your decoy spread, take pains whenever possible to place no decoy beyond 30 or 35 yards. Then, put a single, very distinctive decoy at what you either have measured or believe to be approximately 40 yards from the blind location. In most cases, I'll use a magnum drake pintail decoy as my marker block placed on the downwind edge of my landing zone or hole. First, and unless I'm hunting an area with a wealth of sprig, this decoy will be the only pintail block in my rig. Secondly, the bull sprig's coloration – the white chest and neck – makes this

Closely approximating actual field conditions, sporting clays can be an excellent way to practice and stay in tune during the off-season.

decoy very visible, even under less-than-perfect sighting conditions. Theoretically, any birds decoying within this marker are then within 40 yards, and well within my effective range. Does it work all the time? No, mainly because the birds don't know enough to *always* fly over or near the 40-yard marker decoy. Still, for those birds that do hit the hole into the wind according to the textbook, such a marker can indeed make a difference.

On getting better

All that said, how do you become a better shotgun shooter? In truth, the secret is really no secret at all. It is, however, a three-part process.

The first part is first simply because it's the most important. That is, finding a shotgun that fits you. That's you, not your shooting partner, your son or daughter, your uncle, or the guy down the way. Today, there's absolutely no reason to have a shotgun that doesn't fit. Unfortunately, "fitting" is not how the majority of shotguns come to the shooter from the manufacturer. Rather, these mass-produced firearms are designed to fit what's known as the Universal Human, an individual just under six feet in height, average weight, and an approximately 26 to 28-inch fingertip to armpit reach. Maybe that's you; maybe it's not. Personally, I stand 6'4", weight 190, and have a 31-inch reach and a slender – some would call it downright skinny - build, which means that most shotguns as they come over the counter are stocked some-

what short for a person of my size and shape. When I do find one, like my Remington 11-87, that does indeed fit and fit well, I hang on to it.

Before venturing into shotgun fit a bit further, let me first explain something about a shotgun stock. The purpose of a shotgun stock, other than ensuring the firearm doesn't look aesthetically strange, is in fact the essence behind shotgun fit. A shotgun stock serves as a stationary rest or consistent anchor point for the cheek. Or more importantly, the eye. The eye, then, acts as the shotgun's rear sight in much the same way as a buckhorn or V-notch sight works in conjunction with the bead or post on the muzzle of a centerfire rifle. Should the rear sight or eye not be in perfect alignment, and in perfect alignment every time the firearm is discharged, with the front sight, the result will be inaccuracy. Take, for instance, the archer who anchors his bowstring at the corner of his mouth. If this same archer were to randomly select anchor points - the corner of his mouth, a half-inch above, a half-inch below, the tip of his nose, for example – his shots on target will likewise be all over the place.

What's this all mean? Well, what it means is that in order to achieve the required alignment and consistency, there must first be fit. Lacking fit, the shotgun must *not* fit consistently. Meaning every single time. And here, it becomes apparent that it's much easier to have the gun fit comfortably 100 times in a row than it is to make it not fit the same 100 times.

Here, then, the question turns to the specifics

behind this quest for the Shotgunner's Holy Grail – fit. First, let me say to all the traditionalists out there that the old stand-by method of laying the new shotgun's stock along your forearm, butt in the crock of your elbow, and trigger group somewhere within the boundaries that are your index finger, doesn't mean anything except that the stock measures from your elbow to your fingers. That's it. In days of old, if a person holding a shotgun as such was able to somewhat comfortably curl his trigger finger inside the triggerguard, the shotgun was said "to fit." Today, we can be both more precise and a bit more scientific than that.

The best way to ensure that a new shotgun, or a used one for that matter, will fit is to have yourself and the gun in question measured, and if need be altered or otherwise adjusted, by a qualified gunsmith. The stock altered, that is, not yourself. The key word here is qualified. While living in Washington, I was lucky enough to stumble upon a full-time preacher who referred to himself as The Stock Doctor. And he was. While fitting my wife, Julie, who is 5'2", 120 pounds, and has nowhere near a 28-inch reach, for her new Remington 11-87, the Stock Doctor showed us several hand-crafted pieces he was currently and very lovingly working on, many of which would eventually cost their new owners anywhere from $1,000 to $2,000. When all was said and done, he not only provided Julie with a shotgun that fit her body size and shape perfectly, but had done an immaculate job of fitting and matching the Jones Adjustable Buttplate to the original wood. Several years and a Beretta 390 later, we would find similar craftsmanship and dedication in central Iowa's Bob Lane, a long-time gunsmith and stock fitter whose work was out-shined only by his wonderful personality. The point here is to find a smith who (1) knows what he or she is doing, and (2) can work with you as an individual to arrive at a fowling piece that fits you, and you specifically. In both cases, the measurements, the adjustable buttplate hardware, and the labor combined cost no more than $100 – a very cheap price to pay for consistency and confidence in the field.

Now that you've arrived at a shotgun that truly does fit you, it's time to look at part two of the three-part process. This step involves learning and understanding the capabilities of both your shotgun and the ammunition you've chosen to use in a particular situation. Elemental? Yes, but it's also often overlooked or simply forgotten. Through the process of selecting a gauge, choke, and ammunition combination as outlined earlier in the chapter, you have in essence defined the limitations of your fowling piece. The common denominator here, regardless of the elements which make up this combination, is that the shotgun has been, is, and always will be a short-range firearm. Period. Yes, in the hands of incredible shooters such as Tom Roster, one of the lead-

By making shotgunning practice enjoyable, shooters are more likely to stay active throughout the summer months.

ing developers and testers of today's non-toxic ammunition, the shotgun can become a consistent 50, 60, 70, and perhaps longer-range producer; however, Roster is one man in a million, and most of us, myself included, are only effective and consistent at ranges far less than even Roster's minimum. The concept behind step two is actually very simple. If you know what makes your car operate, and how it will or won't operate well under certain conditions, you will be a better, safer, and more proficient operator of that car. Now substitute "shotgun" for "car," and "shoot" for "operate" and you have the basics of better shotgun shooting.

And finally, there's part three – the simplest, least intimidating, most enjoyable aspect of the entire recipe for improving your shotgunning skills. This miraculous discovery? Practice. And practice. And practice. Only my father, for whatever reason, is capable of putting his shotgun away in mid-January, never touching it again until early goose season in September, and being just as deadly with the piece as he was at the close of the previous year. Okay, so I'm sure there are others; however, these types of individuals are much more the exception rather than the rule when it comes to maintaining or better yet, improving, one's shotgunning skills.

Shotgunning practice can take many forms. Trap, skeet, and sporting clays are but three of the ways that shooters can stay in tip-top shape during the off-season. So, too, can hunts for such challenging winged species as crows, pigeons, or even starlings.

Today, specialty choke tubes designed specifically with the waterfowler in mind are available from a variety of manufacturers including Lohman (black, upright) and Hunter's Specialties.

But as much as it's easy to applaud the positive progress you make as an improving shooter, it's also very important to the continuation of that improvement that you analyze and attempt to correct your shooting faults as well. In other words, it's vital that you recognize the potential for bad habits *before* they actually become bad shooting habits. This applies not only to time spent informally on the trap, skeet, or sporting clays course, but particularly to your shooting habits in the field.

Currently, Iowa City's Phil Bourjaily serves as the shotgun shooting editor for the New York City-based *Field & Stream* magazine. Each month and as part of his journalistic responsibilities for the publication, Bourjaily expounds upon a different issue of the shooting sports; all of which, however, share one common starting point – the shotgun.

Practicing what he preaches, Bourjaily spends at the very least one night each week at a local shooting range. One night, he says, it's trap; the next, skeet. And on those nights when he's feeling particularly adventurous, he'll head to the sporting clays course – it's not a push-over. I've shot it personally – and try his luck at the round disk version of "springing teal," "driven pheasants," and "running rabbits." At times, he reports, he shoots well. Others, not so well. What Bourjaily does do religiously each time he returns from a session is analyze his performance and mentally prepare himself for improvement in the future. But can this self-analysis work in the field instead of the somewhat environmentally-controlled

shooting range? And if so, then, what does he, as an avid and very frequent shooter, feel is the waterfowler's most common shooting mistake? O.K., mistakes?

"A lot of people want to mount the shotgun as soon as they see a duck and then track it, just as if the shotgun were an anti-aircraft gun. All this does is lead to slowing down (the gun barrel or swing) and aiming too much. A lot of people try to measure a lead. Is it 10 or 12 or 15 feet? They try to be too precise here, and again, it slows the gun down. The third mistake I see concerns the fact that the shotgun has got to do what the duck is doing. I mean, if the bird's coming in and dropping, the gun barrel has to start above the bird and come down below it. You just can't stand up and shoot at the duck," said Bourjaily.

But recognizing the problem – "Hi. My name is Bob, and I can't hit the side of a barn." – and correcting the problem or problems are two very different things. According to Bourjaily, though, there is an answer.

"The best thing anyone can do, and I did this last year, is to take a lesson or lessons from a qualified [there's that word again] shooting instructor. That can help you unlearn years and years of bad shooting habits, and teach you the right to do things like how to look at a target, and decide how you're going to shoot it and when you're going to shoot it. An instructor can give you what I'll call a consistent approach to shooting. I had a lesson with Steve Schultz, who's one of the best instructors in the country last year, and it was tremendous," he said.

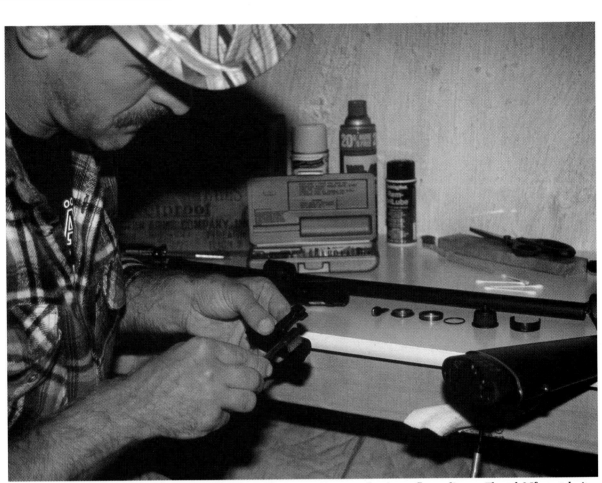

Without question, the most common cause of shotgun malfunction is improper cleaning or flat negligence. The rule? If you take it out, wipe it down. If you shoot it, even once, clean it. Every time.

"That's one thing. Shooting a lot of clay targets is another. There's a lot of people who claim they can't shoot clay targets but they can shoot game. And there's a few people where that's true. But with most people, if they can't shoot clay targets, they can't shoot ducks either," he continued.

This brings up the question, nay the argument, the one that is heard every Saturday morning across the country as shotgunners watch the weekend outdoor shows. "Sure," the television viewers and critics say. "That guy with the fancy gun can shoot all those clay pigeons while it's 75 degrees and sunny. Hell, he's even wearing shorts. You take that guy, wrap him in half the cold-weather clothes that Cabela's makes, throw his butt waist-deep in 40 degree water and blow sleet in his face, and then let's see how many t-a-r-g-e-t-s he's going to hit." According to Bourjaily, it really doesn't matter because chances are, a good shotgun shooter on the range is going to be a good shotgun shooter in the field. Why? Mechanics.

"I don't worry about recreating the field conditions while I practice because I think the important thing is to work on the fundamentals of shooting. Most of us don't have very good shooting fundamentals. You know, practicing in your duck hunting coat and practicing lying on your back and all that other stuff you read about. I don't think that is as important as going out and learning how to properly swing a gun. How to look hard at a target. It's just like a basketball player practicing his jump shot. He doesn't do it with somebody's hand in his face, does he? No, he does it in an empty gym where he can concentrate on his form. I think shooting is the same way," he said.

And there it is. The Secret. The Magic behind successful shotgunning. A shotgun that fits. And practice. Oh, and little bit more practice.

Boats and Blinds

*"Hi. My name is Mike., and I'm a compulsive blind builder.
Actually, I'm more of an arranger and a
re-arranger than I am a builder, but I like to build 'em too."*

Sunrise from a western Iowa marsh. Is there any place finer than a blind at dawn?

The ultimate marsh chair, a lawn chair covered with camouflage netting. It works wonderfully, and the cost? Fifty cents at a flea market.

A nd so went the first-ever meeting of Blind Builders Anonymous, a newly-formed organization dedicated to helping individuals such as myself and the countless tens of thousands of duck hunters across the country with their affliction. What affliction, you ask?

From the very first time that Oog the Caveman hid himself in the reeds at the edge of some prehistoric marsh in hopes of clubbing a mallard, hunters have come to learn, love, and depend upon that most elemental of construction efforts, the duck blind. Like duck decoys, duck blinds have but two reasons for their existence. The first, obviously, is to hide the hunter or hunters from the sharp eyes of their quarry. But it's the second, however, that's often much more important than the first. And that is the blind's ability to offer the hunter something to mess with – read: arrange, rearrange, tear down, straighten, add to, or otherwise change *despite* the fact that absolutely NO change was necessary – during times of little or no duck movement. As with the man who can't leave his decoys alone, so, too, is the lure of the duck blind.

Makes and models

Unfortunately, the word "blind" as it's used by the duck hunter is about as descriptive and informative as is the word "gun." What kind of blind? Is it on land?

Some times the best blind is no blind, but rather staying still and relying on your camouflage.

This hunter lays claim to an old muskrat house during a September teal hunt in eastern Iowa.

Mobility and the art of staying portable, like these Washington gunners moving their hide, can make all the difference.

A well-grassed blind along the Little Sioux River in Iowa. The box is only part of the puzzle; complete camouflage is also important.

Underground? Does it float? Is it the size of a 55-gallon drum, or a buried box car – both of which I've heard are currently employed and serving duty as duck blinds in the northern reaches of Iowa? What is it? And what's it look like?

Once the fact has been established that a structure is indeed a blind used for duck hunting, the nomenclature of that structure can then go in one or more of a thousand different directions; however, like many things, blinds can be classified and sub-classified according to a handful of variables. Although often generalizations, these classifications can help folks, particularly those new to the wonderful world of blind building and placement, decide which type or style of hide is right for their situation.

Permanence, or how long you might expect the blind to remain in any one place or location, is the first consideration. Here, fowlers are given three choices – portable, semi-permanent, and permanent.

Portable blinds are just that – portable – and offer the duck hunter the ultimate in mobility. Say, for instance, you're hunting a 100-acre flooded cornfield. The first day with the wind from the northwest, the small blind you've constructed on the northern edge of the sheetwater worked wonderfully, with the bulk of the birds decoying from the south as they technically should; however, the following day's winds, which are from the southwest, mean that most of the morning's birds will approach your spread from the north. In other words, from behind you. Fortunately, it's a simple matter to col-

lapse your light, two-person tent-like blind of camouflage burlap and PVC poles, and relocate to a southern portion of the field. A few minutes of adjusting cornstalk coverings, and you're back in business. Just try that with a pit blind!

In the past, portable blinds were typically homemade, usually out of lightweight and easily transported materials such as burlap or netting. Stability and structure was provided with similarly light poles made of plastic, wood, or in some cases, aluminum. Today, however, the freelance waterfowler who wants to retain the option of quick and simple blind relocation has at his disposal a variety of commercially manufactured portable blinds. Many of these feature lightweight yet very durable materials such as Cordura nylon or even Kevlar, with most being available in a wide range of popular camouflage patterns. Mail-order houses such as Cabela's or Bass Pro Shops usually carry a selection of these pre-fab portable blinds, as do blind-specific manufacturers such as Oregon's Final Approach Incorporated.

Like portable blinds, semi-permanent hides are most easily defined by name. Though not nearly as mobile as are portables, semi-permanent blinds can nonetheless be moved from place to place and property to property. Often, these movements don't take place until after the close of the season, a time when these structures can either be dismantled and transported, or lifted and relocated as a unit using something like an all-terrain vehicle and a trailer combination. Typically, semi-

Touching up a permanent blind at Washington's Ridgefield National Wildlife Refuge. Most blinds require periodic upkeep in order to ensure their effectiveness.

permanent blinds receive a fresh covering of native materials annually just before the start of the season. Larger than most portable blinds, these semi-permanent structures are usually intended for two or more hunters, their gear, and retrievers.

Permanent blinds are – surprise! – permanent, and while they frequently offer the finest in comfort and concealment, they're also impossible to relocate should such variables as wind direction or bird habits change. To compensate for this seemingly unconquerable negative, fowlers often invest much in the way of scouting and research as a prelude to locating and constructing a permanent blind. Situated and barring any drastic environmental or climactic changes, such blinds are capable of providing excellent gunning over the course of many seasons.

Permanent or stationary blinds as they're sometimes called come in many shapes, sizes, and styles; however, most waterfowlers are familiar with what many consider to head the list in terms of popularity, the pit blind. Essentially little more than a hole in the ground, pit blinds are at times the only option available, particularly in those situations where slight or absent natural cover prohibits hiding above ground. But pits aren't the only type of permanent blind in use today. In some locales, and Tennessee's Reelfoot Lake is an excellent example, permanent house-like or pillbox blinds, many constructed on pilings located at the edges of small stands of flooded timber, are handed down from generation to generation.

The choice as to what type of blind to build and use – portable, semi-permanent, or stationary – is in most cases dictated by variables such as location, access, and land ownership, as well as lesser elements like weather; however, in most cases, the final determining factor as to that style of blind best suited to the situation will indeed by decided by the birds themselves. Elemental? Certainly, but it does absolutely no good to build the Taj Mahal of Duck Blinds if it's not where the ducks want to be.

Blind placement

As I said, it does no good to have the greatest of blinds if it's in the wrong place. Well, then, how do you determine the right place for the blind? Actually, the answer to the blind placement question is easy – Put it where the birds want to be.

It's like this. Decoy spreads and fine calling can indeed convince birds to alter their daily routine. Their pattern, if you will. However, plastic ducks and calling can only do so much, especially if you've put yourself in a location where either the ducks aren't accustomed to being, or, in the worst case scenario, don't want to be at all.

That said, the first step in determining where the blind should be located is an intimate knowledge of the area you're dealing with. What does it look like? How is it shaped? What's the predominant wind direction? Where is the most natural cover? The least? Do you plan

An effective multi-gun blind in use in Washington.

to hunt in the morning? If so, does the blind face east? How about an evening hunt? And finally, are there places on the area to which the birds naturally gravitate? Maybe that's on the lee or off-wind side of a small point. Or maybe there's a small pothole just to the north and east of the main body of water that the birds use throughout the day as a sort of loafing area. Would that be a good spot for a blind, and if so, exactly where along the shore?

For those of you who are thinking that that's a lot of questions but few answers, let's go ahead and take a little more indepth look at those blind placement questions mentioned above. When completed, an examination of such questions will not only provide insight as to where might be the best location for a blind, but will also help answer the question of what kind of blind might work best.

1. **What does the area look like?** While every hunting situation is different in terms of physical appearance and layout, there are some general rules of thumb that blind builders and locators can use to help them get started. One such physical characteristic of concern to blind builders is size; that is, the size of the area being hunted. Maybe one blind isn't sufficient to cover the entire area. If so, perhaps two or even more might be in order.

2. **How is the area shaped?** An area's shape also contributes to blind location. For instance, a long hour

glass-shaped lake – wide at both ends and narrow in the middle – may lend itself well to a blind or blinds on either side of the narrow "straits" in the waist section of the area. Birds working from one end to the other will naturally pass through this sort of funnel, providing both pass-shooting and decoying opportunities. You say you're having trouble locating these 'pinch points' or other geographical possibilities? One tactic that's helped many a hunter determine the best spot for a new blind is through the use of aerial photographs. Certainly, such techniques can be a bit costly; however, there are few finer and more accurate ways of deciding where the birds might best like to be on any given area than by visualizing the ground from a bird's eye view.

3. **What is the predominant wind direction?** Yes, the wind does change; however, most areas in the country will show a predominant wind direction, that compass point from which the wind arrives the vast majority of the time. Blind location as it relates to wind direction takes into account a duck's tendency to land into the wind. Thus, blinds are situated ideally so as to allow the predominant wind to blow from back to front. If that's not possible, side to side is a follow-up, and often just as effective. Least desirable from a directional standpoint is a blind location that puts the predominant wind in the shooter's face. Technically speaking, such a situation will see birds

A little netting, a couple sticks, and a bunch of grass are often all that's needed. Anything more, and it stands out like a sore thumb.

decoying from behind the blind, if they decoy at all (late-season or pressured birds will often show a hesitancy to fly over dry ground adjacent to water, presumably as they 'know' this is where the blinds and therefore the hunters must be). Shots, if they come, in such a case can be difficult to say the least. In our aforementioned hypothetical hour-glass lake situation, let's assume that the predominant wind direction is northwest. Here, the blind on the east point in the middle or 'waist' of the lake will more often receive the lion's share of the attention, with birds decoying from the south into the sheltered waters on the lee side of the point. With a south wind, a properly positioned blind on this same east point can also shoot onto the north or then lee side of the spit. A west wind? Forget it.

4. **Where's the cover?** Natural cover or the lack thereof can also be a factor in the equation that is blind placement. True, it makes perfectly good sense to take advantage of what natural cover, be it cattails, Scotch broom, foxtail, or what have you, exists at the hunting location. Your goal, after all, is to blend into the environment – the natural environment – while making as little a change as possible in what the birds have either grown accustomed to or recognize as insignificant. That's it. You're striving for insignificance. But, too, it doesn't on the other hand make any sense to

plant yourself, figuratively speaking, in the middle of cover so thick as to make shooting or bird retrieval an impossibility. And what about those instances where there is no cover? Blinds of native materials don't necessary have to be built among those same native materials, but can instead be placed within a reasonable distance. Given time, ducks can and will get used to that 'new' clump of cattails or willows; however, the key here is to plan far enough in advance so as to allow time for the birds to get comfortable with this change in their environment.

5. **The sun?** Although sunny, or bluebird days as they're known in the waterfowler's vernacular, are relatively low on the list of desirable climactic conditions - except for those hunting flooded timber where a high, bright sun throws a glare on the water that makes it difficult for the birds to see hunters leaning against their tree-blinds and is therefore a good thing – the sun is nonetheless going to make an appearance at some point during the course of the season. And when it does, it pays to be sitting in a blind that's facing any direction but east. Sometimes, whether due to any of the four conditions already mentioned, it's impossible to face the blind any direction *but* east. In such a case, you'll have to make due with a lower hat brim and greater attention to details when it comes to camouflage. Still, when possible, it is best to put the sun in the bird's face, not yours.

6. **Are the birds there already?** Several years ago, I was fortunate to get permission to hunt a small rock quarry pond in southwestern Washington. During my earliest scouting trips, I discovered that while the bulk of the mallards, sprig, widgeon, and greenwings that frequented the quarry tended to loaf far offshore, there was one shallow cove, little more than a slight indent in the Scotch broom-lined bank, in the northeast corner than always seemed to hold a group or two. On closer examination, I found that the water in this particular corner ranged from 18 inches to three feet in depth – much shallower than the majority of the steep-sloped quarry. Here, the birds had easy access to a wide variety of aquatic plants, as well as a host of invertebrates including fingernail clams, snails, and a type of freshwater shrimp. Armed with this information, picking a spot for a blind on the brush-covered bank nearby was a simple matter, and we enjoyed very good shooting throughout the whole of the season. My point? Instead of trying to lure birds into a location of my choosing, I let them do the choosing. And in essence, the luring.

With a little ingenuity, any boat can be transformed into a duck boat.

The blind proper

Now that you've decided upon a location, and in doing so, a blind type, it's time to get down to the nitty-gritty, the actual construction and camouflaging of the structure. It's been my experience that regardless of size or shape, location or situation, most duck blinds can be described as stick and string structures. Certainly, both sticks and string can and typically do change between designs and, yes, depend upon the circumstances under which the blind is used; still, all blinds do share these two common denominators – stick and string.

What do I mean, stick and string? Simple. Most blinds, at least those which sit on dry or semi-dry ground, consist of four walls, a door, and a roof. With some, these walls are solid, perhaps made of light plywood onto which is tacked clumps of native materials. Cattails, for instance. In other cases, the walls of the blind are actually fashioned of lightweight material, burlap or netting perhaps, which is stretched and secured between four corner posts – the sticks - with the fourth "wall" left open to serve as a door. Like with solid walls, these cloth foundations – the string – are then adorned with natural materials. Often, the materials used along the rear wall of the structure are purposely gathered and placed so as to extend above the top of the cloth or plywood foundation. These flexible materials are then bent over so as to serve as a low-tech roof. Such blinds or reasonable facsimiles thereof are universal, seeing service from coast to coast. Their popularity stems from the fact that each can be tailored to the particular situation at hand, and can address such variables as the aforementioned permanence and size.

A final word on blinds

Where blinds are concerned, I certainly don't wish to appear remiss nor vague in my description or explanation; however, I'm somewhat at a loss in my attempts to communicate "the" perfect or best duck blind, simply because while such a beast might indeed exist (it's unlikely, though), blinds, like the selection and training of a new retriever puppy, is as individual and personalized an undertaking as anything might be. To the waterfowler, the creation of a duck blind is just that – a creation. It's a work of art, a baring to the world at large of one's outdoor soul and skills. Or, as with some hides I've seen, the lack thereof. The existence of a blind proves without question of the existence of the hunter as nest-builder. As architect. And as engineer.

In a recent interview, Phil "The Duck Commander" Robertson probably summed up blinds and blind use as best as anyone can. As masterful with brevity as he is with his Reacher duck call, Robertson put it this way – "You just gotta hide from the ducks." Truth is, that's about all there is to it.

Here, a home-made cover turns an ordinary 14-foot jon-boat into a duck blind. A little natural vegetation, and the effect is complete.

The Ultimate Beast of Burden – Duck Boats

I had to admit – Dave Fountain was right. The monstrosity coming into the ramp at the small public hunting area in eastern Iowa did indeed look like a Viking war ship. Or, as I suggested, a soon-to-be funeral pyre, a tribute, I explained to Fountain, to a mongol's fallen comrade. At either rate, the vessel, with its four-foot-high corrugated tin sides and long, slender oars, which appeared almost magically from holes in the sides of the skiff, did not look the part of a duck boat. All that was lacking, Fountain said with a giggle later, was a wooden naked lady jutting from the craft's aluminum bow and the angry shouts of "Stroke harder, ye swabs." Still, the folks had themselves a duck boat, and from the smiles and lively conversation, they were right proud of their creation. They hadn't, as we were to find out from our brief but very pleasant discussion with them, killed any ducks that morning, a statistic that wasn't entirely surprising given the fact that their boat, easily tall enough for a group of third-graders to hold a sack race in, stood out like a Styrofoam cup in a coal bin.

Jump ahead to another place and time. As my wife and I watch, the small group of sprig – six or eight birds – circle. Lower, then they rise, then it's the long swing that pintails are known for. Below the small group, we can see what looks like a reasonably well-placed spread of decoys; however, there's one thing missing – a blind.

Suddenly, the birds, now not more than 30 yards off the water, tower. One, then another falls. Only then do we notice the gun barrels and the men. From unassuming clumps of smartweed and fall-killed millet, neither more than 18 inches high, they had risen, like camo-clad jacks from their carnival-colored wind-up boxes, each to fill their daily one-bird limit of bull sprig. Voyeurs, we watch through field glasses as one of the men stands, retrieves both birds, and returns to what we've now deduced was as low profile combination boat blinds. The last we see are a few twists, turns, and gyrations as the vegetation displaced is again replaced, and before our eyes, the man – and his boat – vanish. "Impressive," said Julie, my wife. And it was.

The reasons behind the raft

Every waterfowler has his or her own idea of what a "duck boat" is and what it's used for. To Tony Toye, for instance, a young man who guides duck hunters on the Mississippi River and specializes in the hunting and harvest of drake canvasbacks, a duck boat is akin to a floating office, a 20-foot, 90-horsepower home away from home that out of necessity must contain everything needed to get him and his clients to the

The AquaPod, grassed and ready for action.

Lightweight and easily maneuvered, canoes have long been a favorite among freelance waterfowlers coast to coast. *Photo courtesy of Mossy Oak.*

Due to its incredibly low profile, the AquaPod can be used in situations where more traditional boats simply can't go – even in mud.

middle of the river and back safely and successfully. Toye's skiff, a huge flat-bottomed thing, is a masterpiece of modern technology, stealth camouflage, and convenience – right down to the propane cookstove the man uses to prepare hearty breakfasts of bacon and eggs for his folks. On the other end of the country, Washington state's Tony Miller and his son and daughter are right at home in a small 12-foot semi-V powered by a Minn Kota trolling motor and covered with a 15-foot piece of camouflage burlap. Off the coast of North Carolina, there's a 21-foot Boston Whaler, white of all things, that during the winter serves its skipper quite well as blind for his frequent sea duck hunts.

Ever since the first colonial duck hunter stepped into a shaky dug-out canoe and floated downstream into a raft of redheads, thus providing dinner for his family and the families of several other frontiersmen, waterfowlers have come to recognize the importance and potential of the boat as a hunting tool. While virtually anything that floats can in theory be a duck boat, the waterfowl skiffs of today are often high-tech, camouflage-dipped, center console affairs sporting palm frond grass skirts, doggie doors, propane heaters, and sliding overhead doors; still, there are those that revel in heading afield with canoe or jon-boat in tow, and armed with little more than the anticipation that comes with a quiet sojourn down an equally as peaceful stream.

But what boats? Just what do these "holes in the water that you throw money into" do for the duck hunter than he or she can't do without? Essentially, a duck boat performs one of three principle tasks. True, what may start out as one might lead eventually to another, but for the most part, it's one of three.

1. **Access to a permanent blind or offshore hunting area.** In this scenario, the boat is used as a taxi, a means by which the hunter or hunters get from the ramp or another place where hunting isn't taking place to, well, somewhere that it *is* taking place. This might a permanent blind on another section of the lake or river, and perhaps an off-shore island. Maybe it's just to a hole in the timber somewhere along the Cache River in Arkansas. In any case, the boat makes possible that which otherwise wouldn't be.

2. **Floating or jump-shooting.** On moving waters such as rivers or streams, boats, often canoes or smaller skiffs, are used to slowly and quietly float along, the intent being to sneak up and surprise ducks which are sitting hidden around the river's many twists and turns. Often, these boats are camouflaged to resemble a pile of branches, leaves, or other common waterside flotsom – something that might naturally be seen floating downstream after becoming dislodged from the bank.

Commerically-made camouflage boat blinds, or covers, like this one available from Avery Outdoors are another option available to the duck boater. *Photo courtesy of Avery Outdoors.*

3. **Hiding.** Finally, there are the boat blinds. These are those watercraft that serve both as aquatic conveyance and hiding place, all in one neatly camouflaged and motorized – or at least powered in some fashion – package. These types of boat/blind combinations are particularly popular along many of the nation's major river systems such as the Missouri, the Mississippi, and the Columbia, as well as on any number of larger inland lakes such as the Great Salt Lake in Utah or Missouri's Lake of the Ozarks.

The AquaPod by ATTBAR, Inc., one of the best duck boats on the market today, and a must for the freelancer looking for something new.

4. **The miscellaneous.** Like the differences between breeds of dogs, there are often great degrees of variation between the different types of duck boats. Enough, perhaps, to warrant the subject worthy of its very own book. Or at least its own chapter. There are, for instance, other smaller boats that aren't canoes and yet aren't of your traditional flat-bottom or V-hull design. Such a category might include layout or sculling boats, two very traditional oar-powered skiffs popular among the diving duck hunting crowd along the Great Lakes and the Eastern Seaboard. Too, this same category might include hybrids such as the AquaPod, a fiberglass wonder that has a keel, thus setting it apart from the stationary non-keeled layout boats, and uses a double-bladed kayak style paddle, an implement that distinguishes the Pod from the rear-oared scull boat. Then there's the Outlaw

Ducker, an olive-drab, outboard driven skiff that looks like someone hung a motor on a giant green Good 'n Plenty, and yet a boat that many gunners in the Pacific Northwest swear by. The bottom line is there is no bottom line. Boats, like blinds, are as individual as their owners. If it works, it works – even if it's a discarded Maytag refrigerator door built for three – Dad's seen it, and swears it's true!

Friends

"The man who talks to himself is crazy. But if he talks to his dog, he's a conversationalist" – Jim Schoby on why it's all right to talk to your dog in the duck blind.

There's always room on the bench for a buddy

The stories are endless. They are timeless.

No judge. No jury. No shooting critic. Their fee, a pat – a hug – a hastily thrown piece of driftwood. Theirs is a world of compromise. Of "are you happy?" Ask a man to define his life, and you will have words for all. Ask that man, that waterfowler, of his favorite hound, and you will have a moment of silence. And an infinite look into that place where memories live forever.

Here, let the old adage, "a picture is worth a thousand words" earn it's keep.

Impossible retrieves. Narrow escapes. Puppies. Backyard kennels.

Ours would be a much lonelier, a much colder world if it weren't for the wealth of nuzzles and pats, scratches and deep-throated "he's just happy" growls.

And ours is a soul-shatteringly empty place when one passes on.
We speak fondly. And cry. And next year we'll watch the sky...

...and smile at the insistant nudges from a cold, wet nose. And strong hearted future.

Calling all Birds

"A duck call in the hands of the unskilled is conservation's greatest asset" – Nash Buckingham, legendary outdoor writer

"Friends don't let friends have duck calls." – unknown duck hunter at Washington state check station

The essence of duck calling: Where to begin

First let me start off by saying something that might surprise some of you given its source is the author of a book on duck hunting. I am a mediocre duck caller. Not good, but not bad. And the reasons for this are several.

Although raised by a duck hunter, I was not raised by a duck caller. Sure, my father had a duck call, a now antique Olt Model D-2. And yes, it was carried into the field; however, other than the traditional pre-season "let's see if this thing still works" quack or two, the Olt was never put to his lips. Eventually, I inherited the call, and have it today, although even by my average-guy standards, it sounds pretty bad.

Secondly, there really was no need to attempt to call ducks during my formative years. You see, in the mid-1970s, there were lots of ducks, and if one bunch wouldn't pay any attention to our little slice of avian heaven there at Wolfe's Swamp or Roper's or Simmons', well, it wouldn't be long before another bunch that was interested would come along and drop right in. Too, we hunted small beaver swamps and patches of flooded pin oaks, and it was seldom that the mallards and wood ducks didn't trip over themselves in order to be the first bird on the water. Oh, I figure that some calling, even mediocre calling, would have helped convince those passers-by that

where we were was indeed the place to be; however, like many, if the Old Man – that's a term of endearment in my eyes – didn't need to do it, then I didn't need to either.

Over time, though, as I progressed through the first two or three steps in my hunting career and finally arrived at the technique or methodology stage, I realized that there was something more to this duck calling thing than, well, simply not using one. The fact that I was introduced to the sport of turkey hunting, and therefore turkey calling, in the late 1980s might have had something to do with my revelation, and I began to look at these calls as quite possibly a useful tool, something to be studied and practiced and implemented rather than a frightening or intimidating piece of duck hunting hardware.

Still, and despite several years now of calls and calling, I wasn't sure if I was, for lack of a better term, qualified to write about this very important aspect of duck hunting. Fortunately for me, I knew someone who was.

At 50, Buck Gardner is a duck hunter's duck hunter.

"My Dad, Arch, took me (duck hunting) when I was six years old. I wore the hip boots that I got for Christmas that year, and went in over my head retrieving two little wood ducks. I guess that was my baptism. And I've been going ever since," said Gardner. "He's 84 now, but my Dad still goes with me, and my Mom still cooks what we bring home."

To Gardner, a duck call and the art that is calling ducks have always been magical things. Since his introduction to the sport in the mid-1950s, Gardner has practiced and preached and perfected his calling skills and

Duck calls and duck calling introduce a fascinating element into an already intriguing art form.

techniques to where today, his playing of his own brand of musical instrument is akin to, say, B.B. King's relationship with Lucille, or Louie Armstrong's way with that beautiful piece of brass. It's music, plain and simple.

"My Dad started me calling when I was 6 by sending me outside to go let off some steam and blow a duck call. I thought I knew it all by the time I was 16. I blew in my first contest in the Alabama State Championship in 1980, and got disqualified for talking to the emcee. Came in last!" said Gardner.

Disappointed but not discouraged, Gardner turned this first negative experience into something good, and proved that practice and perseverance pay off by winning the Alabama State Contest in 1981. That same year, he placed fifth in the World competition in Stuttgart, Arkansas. The next year, the young caller won the Mississippi Delta Regional contest, at that time the largest regional competition held. Finally in 1994, Gardner's hard work paid off in spades as he walked away with the coveted World Championship ring, all this after placing third three times and finishing among the world's finest in an astounding seven contests. But the young man wasn't finished as the following year he won the title of Champion of Champions, a competition open only to World Champions and held only every five years.

"With that, I finished my competitive calling career. If you have to go out, it's best to go out on top," said Gardner, whose calling resume' also includes the

Alabama State Title (3), Tennessee State Title (3), Mississippi Delta Regional (3), Music City Regional (2), the Heart of Dixie Regional (1), Eastern Kansas Open (1), and, as he says with a smile, "something else twice."

Now that he's hung up his competition calling hat, Gardner spends much of his time – retirement, he calls it – doing a little consulting work, a whole lot of hunting, and even more time teaching folks, especially young people, how to make music with a piece of acrylic plastic or wood and a couple thin reeds. And like watching Olympic figure skaters, Gardner makes it look easy.

Step 1 – Choosing the right call

Just like Tiger Woods needs clubs that fit, and Emeril Legasse needs a hot skillet and a little bit of essence, a duck caller should have the right call. And what's the right call? Well, according to Gardner, the right call can be a lot of different things; however, there are some encouraging notes for those first-timers who have all but been scared when confronted with rack upon rack upon rack of duck calls. There's blue ones and red ones, camouflage ones and those with little brass rings. There's duck calls with one reed, and calls with two. And as if the colors or reed configurations aren't enough to drive a holy man to drink, there's an infinite list of interesting and provocative names like the

World Champion and Champion of Champions, Buck Gardner, one of the best in the business.

Duck calling is something learned over a period of years. 26 years, and I'm still learning.

Wench, the Timber Wench, the Sweet Talker, the Variable Red Leg, and the Sweet Susie. How's a man to tell one from the other?

"Today, there truly are a lot of good calls in the marketplace. It's much easier today to get a good product to work with than it used to be. The calls themselves have improved tremendously," said Gardner. "Most people are attracted by the look of a call. You want to find something that you like the way it looks and it's comfortable in your hand. Also, the way the call feels and fits to your lips. Some people make calls with real sharp edges. And quite frankly, if you're going to be blowing one a lot, a sharp-edged mouthpiece gets very old. Some people make one that has a flared barrel on it. Again, that gets uncomfortable after a while."

Looks, fit, and feel are but three parts of the entire call equation, says Gardner. There's still the question of whether or not the call can and will stand up to the potential punishment and flat-out abuse commonly given equipment housed in a blind or boat.

"Is it durable? Is it made out of a product that looks like it's going to hold up to some rugged use? The last thing you want to have happen is that you're out hunting somewhere and everything's good, and you drop your call or you bump it, and it breaks and cracks and is no longer functional. You want a call that's sturdy," he said.

Essentially, you're going to have to choose between calls with one reed and those with two. Single reed calls, surprisingly enough, are the more difficult of the two to

Traditionally, most American duck callers have started their education with mallards, as this hunter demonstrates. *Photo courtesy of Mossy Oak.*

On big waters like the Mississippi, volume plays a vital role in gaining the birds' attention. Here, river guide Tony Toye hopes to turn some heads – duck heads, that is.

learn and master. This is, as Gardner says, because you have one reed that's being asked to do everything from a high pitch to a low pitch. With single reed calls, factors such as air and tongue control become very, very important in getting the call to function properly. Two reeded calls, on the other hand, are a bit more forgiving, particularly to the inexperienced.

"A single reed call is really just like a musical instrument. They're just a little harder to blow. Two reeds, when you lay one on top of the other, well, they won't go as high on the high end or as low on the low end. A double reed call won't squeak on the top, and tends to blow easier for the guy who doesn't know how to put duck sounds into a call," said Gardner.

Oh, and as for color, Gardner says that a duck call's little different than a crankbait.

"The colored calls are made just so people will buy them. It's just like fishing lures that are brightly colored. You know, first you have to catch the fisherman (he laughs). First you have to catch the duck hunter. And personally I like to tell people that if a duck gets close enough to see that brass band on my duck call and have that bother him, generally I can kill him. It's just really a preference as to what the consumer wants," he said.

Step 2 – Learning duck talk

Once you've taken the plunge and bought Duck Call

X, the next step becomes learning to use it to create sounds that are natural and realistic as opposed to frightening and spine-twisting. I'm a firm believer in a four-part process –

1. **Buy an instructional audio** cassette tape or CD, and listen to it. Listen to it over and over and over. Learn every break and breath and phase. Videos are available and can work; however, with audio tapes, you only have to listen. Once you get your eyes involved with something like a video, your brain can't help but get distracted. Get a tape, close your eyes – unless, that is, you're learning on the freeway on the ride home from work – and listen. Gardner, by the way, narrates and leads one of the best instructional tapes on duck calling, *Straight Talk*, available today.

2. **Go to the closest city park** and listen to the ducks. Pay attention to what they're doing physically while they're calling. Are there ducks in the air? If so, how are they calling to them? Do they call a little, or a lot? And what about volume? Learn the differences between the sounds made by drakes and hens. Although it's traditional and much more common to call as a hen, particularly a mallard hen, there's times when using alternative calls such as the sounds made by drake mallards, green-wing teal, gadwall, or widgeon can be very effective. In the next chap-

ter, Phil Robertson discusses these alternative calls in much greater detail.

3. **Find an experienced caller** and recruit him or her as your mentor and tutor. Most duck hunters are more than happy to spend time helping a new caller. And besides, it provides them an opportunity to puff out their chest and show off a bit. Such experience can often be tracked down at a local sporting goods shop, or better yet, a function sponsored by Delta Waterfowl, Ducks Unlimited, or any of the many state and regional waterfowl and wetlands conservation organizations. The trick here is to not be afraid to try, to ask questions, and most importantly, practice.

4. **Eventually, you'll come full circle,** and here's where Gardner suggests making a personal demo tape of yourself going through a calling sequence. Listen to the tape yourself, and grade or critique your performance. Next, give the tape to your mentor/tutor, and ask them to do the same. Remind them that they need to be brutally honest in their appraisal of your calling, as kind words may be easy on the heart and soul, but they're not going to do a damn thing for you if your duck calling's lousy.

Step 3 – A calling sequence, ala' Gardner

Although practice never ends when it comes to perfecting your duck calling, sooner or later you're going to have to step outside your office or truck, put on your waders, and take all that you've learned into the field. That's difficult, you say, because while you've learned to make, and quite well you quickly add, the various types of calls, you're not entirely sure when to use them or what response – really – they're supposed to elicit in the field.

Fortunately, and while the whole of a hen mallard's vocabulary remains a mystery, there are just four basic calls which are made at four basic times during a duck's or a flock of ducks' approach to or departure from the blind location. These are the hail or greeting call, the intermediate greeting call, the feeding chuckle or variations thereof, and the comeback call.

The hail or greeting call

"When ducks are way off in the distance, and I mean 600 to 800 yards and they're downwind and they can hear you, you want to make a hail call or greeting call. It's a long loud call that a duck can't (physically) do. The purpose is strictly to get their attention. The ducks might

"You put the call up to your lips, just like you're taking a drink from a Coca-Cola bottle," says Buck Gardner, shown here doing what he does best.

not even be thinking about coming over where you are, and you have to do something to get those ducks' attention. It's a long cadence from 8-15 notes," said Gardner. "They don't hear all the notes. They just hear some of them," he continued.

Phonetically, the hail call would look something like

Q—U—A—C—K...Q—U—A—C—K...Q—U—A—C—K...Q-U-A-C-K..Q-U-A-C-K..Q-U-A-C-K..Q-U-A-C-K..QUACK..QUACK..QUACK..QUACK..QUACK.

Imagine that you're the quarterback of a professional football team. You're at one goal line, and your favorite receiver is standing at the other – 100 yards away. He's looking up into the stands, searching perhaps for the beer vendor. How do you get his attention from that distance? You yell. That's the hail call.

The intermediate greeting call

"As the ducks come to you," says Gardner, "you'll continue with a more excited greeting call. Sound excited. Once a duck gets within 100-150 yards, you need to start making sounds that a duck can make. And the reason is, is that they can hear pretty much everything you do. And the thing that causes people the biggest problem is they call ducks from a distance and they get (the ducks) close, and then the ducks figure out, 'Hey, that's somebody blowing a duck call. That ain't ducks.' Some folks call it over-calling. Well, it's not so much over-calling. It's just that the ducks figure out that you're not

Lanyards help keep the hunter's calls organized and handy.

doing what a duck does."

As Gardner says, the intermediate greeting call is nothing more than a spiced-up version of the hail call. Simply turn down the volume to match the distance from yourself to the birds, and pick up the excitement and intensity a bit. What you're saying to the birds is 'Hey, this IS the place to be. Come on over, and make it snappy.'

Remember your receiver? Well, he not only heard you, but he's now at the 40-yard line and coming to see what you want. No need to yell now, but you're glad he's coming over.

The (infamous) feeding chuckle

If you're a duck hunter, even with only one season under your belt, I'm sure you've heard a neighbor doing the feeding chuckle. It's that rapid, machine-gun yammering that sounds a bit like muted milk bottles riding in the back of a panel van over 50 miles of mild washboard. In the worst scenarios, change the washboard to railroad tracks, and you have the ultimate in mind-altering noise.

In its purest form, the feeding chuckle is supposed to reproduce the continuous rolling audio undertone that's made when ducks gather to feed. It's a sound of contentment, like the soft purr and whine of a hen turkey, the purr of a cat, or those low, back-of-the-throat "rawr, rawr, rawr" sounds your black lab makes

when you scratch his belly. Now imagine two dozen black labs, all having their bellies rubbed simultaneously, each "rawr, rawr-ing" and drooling, and you have the feeding chuckle.

The true chuckle, however, is not an on-the-water sound, but instead is used by a member of a flock of mallards, typically a hen, to keep the rest of the flock organized as they fly high overhead from one spot to another. Still, many duck callers insist on performing this high-altitude vocalization from their hiding spot in the bullrushes. And why do most hunters make this non-stop "ticka-ticka-ticka-ticka-ticka" sound? Because they can.

"When those ducks get within 125-150 yards, you want to go to sounding like a duck. As they come in, you can feed call to them IF you're in an area where ducks would feed. If you're not in an area where ducks would feed, like deep water or where those ducks can't tip up, and you're feed calling to them, quite frankly, I think those ducks go 'Hey, wait a minute. How come they're feed calling down there when they can't eat there?' You gotta make it sound natural and real," says Gardner.

Real and natural. That's the key, and in terms of a feed chuckle, real and natural means riffs of broken, very choppy notes and series of notes, some of which may be brief runs of what sound like the flying chuckle. Again, phonetically –

Tic..ticka-tic..tic..tic..ticka..tic..ticka-ticka-ticka-ticka…
QUACK-QUack-Quack-quack-quack..ticka..ticka-tic –

And so on and so on. With two or more callers calling at the same time, the feeding chuckle outlined above can and often does begin to sound like the unbroken, machine-gun version made by high-flying birds; however, there is a definite difference, one that can often be easily heard when listening to live ducks at the aforementioned city park pond.

As for our receiver, he and his nine partners now surround the quarterback in the huddle. With this being a scrimmage, everyone contributes to the play strategy. Voices rise and fall, and suggestions are made – some strongly, with each player adding to the constant drone of sound. That's a feeding chuckle.

The comeback call

Regardless of how real a decoy spread might look or how well-hidden you and your partners might be, there's times when the ducks for whatever reason decide they don't like what they see and start to leave. Time to give up? Not according to Gardner.

"The call you make then is one of the, if not the, most important call you make. That's the comeback call.

And most people don't use it or work it enough on ducks. The comeback call is kinda like the hail call, but it's urgent and more excited. Basically, it goes 'demand, plead, and beg,'" said Gardner.

Gardner maintains that when the ducks first turn to leave, you should deliver the comeback call as a demand, a firm, no questions here statement that says, 'HEY! DUCKS! Y'all really need to come back here and check this out again.' Sometimes they do, and sometimes they don't. If they don't, then it's time to plead with them. This version of the comeback call, personified, might go something like – 'Aw come on guys! You really need…yes, you really need to come back here and settle down for a spell.'

And if that doesn't do the trick, well then it's time to pull out all the stops and get down to some flat-out begging – 'But…but…but…but….guys. Come on, guys. You don't wanna do that. Guys…hey, guys….aw, come on. Come on, guys. Come on back here.' At this point, one of three things is going to happen. One, the ducks are indeed going to turn back around, at which point you'll go back to the mixture of greeting calls and choppy feed chuckles. Two, the ducks will go away for good. Or three, you'll run out of air, turn blue in the face, and faint into your cold roast beef sandwich. Don't laugh. I've seen it happen.

Ask any duck caller, and chances are he'll agree that calling is not THE answer nor is it a cure-all. It won't cover up mistakes in concealment, and it won't change the fact that your blind is in the wrong location. It won't take the mud off of decoys or make the party who set up

An early morning serenade on the South Platte River in Colorado. Will they come?

100 yards away just as shooting time rolled around disappear. It can, however, be a useful tool – a piece of the entire illusion which you as the waterfowler are trying to create as realistically and naturally as possible.

And besides, blowing a duck call gives you something to do when the birds aren't flying.

Beyond Mallards:
Calling Other Species

Sometimes it's "The Look" that first captures your attention and your interest. Phil Robertson has The Look.

To put it most elementally, Robertson is duck hunting personified. It's not because his company, Duck Commander Products, has been producing some of the country's most popular duck calls and waterfowl hunting paraphernalia since the early 1970s. And it's not due to the fact that Robertson, his wife, and his hunting partners call northern Louisiana, also known as Duckland, home. And surprisingly enough, it's not the black beard sprinkled with white nor the Browning Gold nor the Labrador retriever named Recoil, although certainly, all those variables do play a role.

It's because when you look at him, you know that Phil Robertson *is* a duck hunter. Plain and simple. With a glance, it's obvious that Robertson's dark eyes have searched a million miles of sky, and seen a thousand things that only those who have greeted the new day waist-deep in the marsh have the good fortune – no, the privilege – to witness. His hands have carved more than three decades worth of wood, transforming on a daily basis once ordinary blocks of timber into instruments worthy both of his name and his reputation. Robertson's livelihood, and more significantly, his life, revolves around waterfowl. At the core of the man's existence are fall migrations, fast-flying knots of green-wing teal, squealing summer ducks, and, of course, back-peddling flocks of red-leg mallards. Thus, over the course of more than 40 years, he has earned himself a legacy and a name – The Duck Commander.

A month ago, I had the opportunity to spend the better part of 90 minutes on the telephone with Robertson. And during that all-too-brief time, I learned a lifetime's worth of waterfowl hunting tips and tactics, the most surprising of which was the fact that, despite mak-

ing his living building and selling duck calls, Robertson ranks the fine art of duck calling "eighth" on his list of waterfowling rules, a list known simply as The Duck Commander's "Ten Commandments for Successful Duck Hunting." Eighth, I asked?

"You need to have done your preliminary work. By that, I mean be in the general area where ducks fly over. Next, be in the exact spot where they tend to want to go. And then you get into camouflage and decoy placement. I make a video that's called the Ten Commandments, and I line out these factors. There's 10 factors, and if those 10 factors are in place, well, your duck call is about eighth on the list," said Robertson.

And even at that, Robertson cautions and reminds hunters that successful duck calling needs to be done in moderation.

"What you're trying to do is to mimic exactly what an old hen (mallard) would do. And if you call at the proper time and don't over-do it, day in and day out, it will pay off and you will be more successful. That's just the bottom line to it. Most people over-do everything here in America, and duck calling is just one more thing. They over-do it," he said.

More than mallards

Anyone who has ever watched one of the videos in Robertson's "Duckmen" hunting series will quickly come to the realization – and here's where I'll raise a few hackles - that unlike many waterfowling purists, Robertson and his partners don't concentrate their gunning efforts ONLY on mallards. Certainly, a limit of northern Louisiana drake mallards looks fantastic on a duck hunting video jacket or gracing the front cover of any of the nation's prestigious hunting publications, and, yes, the mallard's table ranking rates among even Robertson's top three (green-wing teal and wood ducks held the number

Pintails, like the beautiful bull sprig, are just one of the many species that can be successfully called using "non-mallard" techniques.

Pintails and gadwalls alike will often respond well to the sounds made by their own kind.

Wood ducks can be a fickle breed when it comes to calling. Sometimes they'll come; often, they won't. But it never hurts to try.

one and number two positions), but mallards aren't the only game in town when it comes to field research for Phil and his Duckmen.

So with this most eclectic harvest by species in mind, I asked The Duck Commander about calls and calling techniques for ducks other than mallards. For my benefit, Robertson did his calling demonstrations with his natural voice, and I've tried to reproduce them phonetically here for the sake of visualization and understanding.

Whistlers – pintails and widgeon

"A pintail drake makes kind of a growling sound, so we'll do a little of that. And we're also doing his whistle. Course, a pintail's pretty slick. We made a policy on the pintails. Usually, their first pass (over the decoys) is their closest one, especially if it's a big bunch, like 40 or 50 birds. Pintails tend to be some of the spookiest (ducks) there are, so if they come within gunshot range, we go ahead and cut 'em. But, yeah, generally we use the whistles," said Robertson.

Like pintails, widgeon can be awfully skittish. Basically flighty, and often very nervous; however, they are a very vocal bird, and it's relatively easy to imitate their simple two or three-note whistling call with any number of devices. For years, I used an ordinary dog whistle whenever the situation called for calling widgeon. Some folks say it's necessary to remove the 'pea' inside the whis-

A hen blue-wing teal produces a quick, high-pitched hen mallard-esque type of quack, a sound which can be deadly on these fast-flying little ducks.

tle before it will work properly on widgeon. Rather than do this, I merely turned the call upside-down and played it that way, and never did have any problem. Others, my wife being one, used their natural voice to whistle in bald-pate, while still others opted for a more conventional – and specific – widgeon call, just like the one marketed by Robertson's outfit. The nice thing about most widgeon calls, other than the typically low price, is the fact that this very elemental call can also be used for calling pintails, drake mallards, and green-wing teal, as well as bobwhite quail. They do an awful good imitation of a red-tailed hawk's screaming cry, too – an excellent locator call for those who enjoy spring turkey hunting.

A widgeon's whistle differs from the pintail's in that it's a clearer, purer sound, and lacks the trilling notes or buzz commonly associated with the drake sprig. Phonetically, the widgeon's call sounds like "woo, whIT, woo," with each sound or word being produced in a breathy, back-of-the-throat sort of way. The drake also makes a very similar two-note whistle – "whIT, woo" – that's easy to reproduce, and can often be heard when the birds are at rest on the water.

Gadwalls, or gray ducks

"(My son) and I came up with this gadwall drake, and that really helped us with the gadwalls. A gadwall hen sounds pretty well like a mallard hen, but the tempo

Available from several different manufacturers, whistles like the one this gunner's using can reproduce a variety of duck calls including pintails, widgeon, teal, and wood ducks.

A dozen decoys and a few quick choppy quacks were all this hunter needed to dupe this early September blue-wing.

Like their blue-winged counterparts, green-wing teal can also prove gullible for the caller using a specialized teal call.

is a little faster and maybe a little more, well, there's not as much body to it. Most people will tell you that a hen gadwall is a mallard hen, but there is a difference to it. And when you mix in that old gadwall – 'bink, bink-bink, bink' – that little sound that they make, well it's a deadly combo, my man," he said.

I killed my first gadwall, a beautiful late-season drake, while hunting the Ridgefield National Wildlife Refuge in southwestern Washington in 1994. Since then, I've had the opportunity to call several dozen grey ducks to my life list, and can't for the life of me figure out why the entire country isn't absolutely head over heels in love with this wonderful duck. First, gadwall seem almost unable to stay out of decoy spreads, particularly when the aforementioned rig is complemented with even mediocre calling. Now, let me say that not all grey ducks are push-overs, only that they rank reasonably high on the willingness scale. Secondly, gadwall are relatively big ducks, comparable in size and weight to a widgeon, or in larger birds, even to sprig. Grey ducks are a handsome bird, especially later in the season when the drakes are wearing their best breeding plumage, and make very interesting and eye-catching mounts for those who fancy such things. And finally, they're more than adequate on the table; perhaps not on a par with a roasted green-wing teal or baked wood duck, but as good or better – my opinion – as any mallard, widgeon, or sprig. And a hell of a lot better than any shoveler, although, and no disrespect to the large-billed bird, that's not saying much.

True or False – Wood duck calls work?

"Wood ducks themselves are among the most difficult ducks to call. Here is what is true. Wood ducks are called much easier if they're already sitting out there. And by that I mean, it's easier to get a wood duck – with a wood duck call, now – to swim to you than (it is) to get him to fly to you. What most people don't realize is that if a wood duck is flying, it's got a 'creeeek – creeeek – creeeek' call. It's a flying call. But when they're sitting on the water, it's a totally different sound. So they have a sound they make when they're flying, which is what you don't want to do because if they're flying and you give them a flying call, nobody knows where to come back to," said Robertson.

The wood duck's vocabulary includes some of the strangest sounds to ever echo over the marsh. Both the hens and the drakes will make a rising whistle or creaking sound, something like an old rusty gate opening or blowing shut in the wind. Add to this a long list of peeps, whines, and low growls, and you start to accumulate a sound track that would rival any B-grade horror movie. More than one waterfowling newcomer has given serious thought to walking out to the edge of the swamp in the black-grey minutes just before shooting time once the wood ducks have started calling to one another. And that's exactly what the birds are doing – calling back and forth in order to locate one another. Often, there will be a noticeable increase in both the frequency and volume of

Opening morning on the South Platte. Callers best be ready, as it's time for the show to begin in earnest.

the calling just before the birds, or several small groups of birds, rise for the morning's flight, and hunter's can use this upswing in audio activity as a warning to get ready for what is often some of the toughest and most challenging wingshooting to be found in the U.S.

Growing up in the northeastern corner of Ohio with both an abundance of wood ducks and a like number of experimental wood duck calls, it's been my experience that 99.9998 percent of the nation's wood duck population will totally ignore a wood duck call; however, I have on at least one occasion seen a small flock of woodies suddenly change course and return to a small timbered pothole where a cousin of mine, wood duck call in hand, had just called to them in their 'peet – w-o-o-O-O-I-T' rising whistle. Coincidence? Perhaps, but it was enough to make a believer out of my cousin, Jimmy, and evidence enough to convince me that on that one-in-a-million occasion when a flying wood duck wants to listen, he will. Otherwise, I'm relatively sure that they're deaf.

Teal – Tops on the table

"The green-wing drake has the 'peep.' It's just peep – peep. Just a little peep. One little whistle, and a kind of low whistle. And we built a little hen teal call that's basically 'teeeeet, teet-teet-teet.'" (NOTE: Imagine a hen mallard's quack, only a higher pitch and faster cadence.) It's only five or six real quick notes. And the blue-wing is

very similar to it, but maybe more of a "burrrrrt, burt, burt, burt." (NOTE: Slower cadence, and slightly lower pitch than the green-wing). The blue-wing responds great to a little hen teal call. And the green-wings, too. I mean they'll turn on a dime. If a man's hunting where there are green-wing or blue-wing teal, you just hafta have you a little teal call – that's all there is to it. It'll help you greatly," he said.

Although I've hunted teal for some 25 years now, both during the early September seasons and throughout the traditional fall months, it's only been within the past two years that I made a concerted attempt to call to them; that is, with something other than a mallard-type call. And while my experiments with a blue-wing teal call in eastern Iowa during the 2000 season were far from conclusive, I will say this – when a teal call works, which it seemed to do about 25 to 30 percent of the time, it worked as well as any live decoy ever could. On several occasions, my wife and I watched small flocks of blue-wings change direction so quickly and so radically after we'd called to them, we were absolutely certain that the little ducks would come into the decoys buck-naked, their feathers having been ripped from their bodies with the G-forces involved with such maneuvers. Other times the speedy little ducks appeared to be almost wood duck-like in their indifference, and seemed almost to be making an effort to ignore our quick, buzzy, high-pitched 'q-u-a-c-k, quack, quack, quack, quack, quack.' The bottom line when it comes to calling teal? It can't hurt.

Moving Water Mixed Bag

The story actually starts the day before the hunt – and I mean in capital letters, THE HUNT – took place. On that particular day in late November, Joe Hassman, a waterfowling cohort of mine, and I had, well before daylight, parked my father's Ford pickup near the boat ramp at a small city park in my hometown of Newton Falls, Ohio. Within minutes we were launching our borrowed canoe – we borrowed a lot of things back then – at a livery on the Mahoning River a short distance downstream from the dam at Lake Milton. The plan was to float the river, stopping here and there, before picking up in Newton Falls.

We didn't get far. Not 300 yards from the launch, a flock of 50 or so mallards took flight, startled as we slid the canoe silently around the inside curve of the bend. "Let's pull over here," I told Hassman. "We'll put out a dozen decoys, and see what happens." Quick to agree, Hassman went to work camouflaging the canoe and building our impromptu hide while I arranged a handful of magnum mallard block in the shallow riffle in front of our position.

The wait wasn't long. Within minutes, a small group of mixed mallards and black ducks appeared over the oaks lining the opposite side of the river, and, with wings cupped, began to slip-slide into the hole I had just created. Six shots later, I was quickly sloshing my way downstream, trying in vain to catch up with the final bird of the two doubles that had involuntarily stayed behind. "Come on," shouted Hassman, "we'll get it with the boat."

Satisfied that our plan had worked to perfection, we dismantled our blind and shoved off downriver to retrieve our last bird. Comparatively speaking, the rest of the trip was rather uneventful; however, the events of the past hours had sparked an idea.

The next morning found us again at the small livery below the Lake Milton Dam; however, this time we had one fewer truck, and planned only to go as far as the site of the previous day's hunt. Even in the darkness as we launched the same borrowed canoe, we could hear birds trading back and forth between the open waters of the lake and the countless riffles and pools on the Mahoning downstream. No two people ever paddled a canoe up to planing speed more quickly than did Hassman and I, eager as we were to see if our choice of stopping points had indeed been a brainstorm worthy of repeating through the ages, or merely a fluke.

We needn't have worried. Like a carbon copy of the morning before, it took only minutes after legal shooting time arrived for small groups of mallards to begin working our small riffle. With flocks landing both upstream and downstream of our location, as well as in the cut corn stubble in front of and behind us, calling became a somewhat moot point. Nonetheless, and in part in an effort to make the hunt last as long as possible, Hassman and I traded off between shooting and calling, only taking one bird from each flock, and only a drake mallard. Still, it took less than two hours before we again found ourselves at the livery, the bottom of the canoe graced by five drake mallards and one of the most beautiful drake black ducks either of us had ever seen. It had truly been a morning to remember for both of us, a morning made possible due to that fact, as Hassman reminded me several times throughout the day, that moving water means mallards.

The moving water equation

Successfully hunting ducks over moving water means recognizing three variables, all three being very important parts of the whole equation. The first of these, and probably the most elemental, is a definition of what constitutes moving water. Essentially, 'moving water' by my definition refers to any body of water possessing a cur-

The Mahoning River in northeastern Ohio provided this brace of drake mallards for this late-season river gunner.

Shallow rivers like the South Platte pictured here are natural hotspots during the late season.

A slough on the Columbia River in Washington state, a hard-to-hunt area due to the twice daily tidal fluctuations; however, this hunter didn't seem to mind the extra work.

rent, be it horizontal or vertical current. These waters can be as large as the Mississippi or the Missouri rivers, or as small as a creek or stream no more than eight or 10 feet across. Currents and current strength, too, can differ, and often does – greatly – ranging from the turbulence of the Columbia River to a barely discernible trickle proved only by the gentle side-to-side waving of submerged grasses. Here, size really doesn't matter. Over the years and many more times than I care to count, I've found several limits of ducks, particularly mallards and secretive wood ducks, paddling around on creeks – proper pronunciation: crick – narrow to the point where the goldenrod on one side practically brushed the 'rod on the other; still, for whatever reason and one in all likelihood known only to the birds themselves, these small insignificant wetlands can at times prove the hottest ticket around.

This definition brings up another important point about moving water. Most everyone is familiar with horizontal current, or the directional movement of water in a river, for instance; however, what many people don't realize when the conversation turns 'round to hunting moving water is that such a category should also include those waters which are tidally influenced. Basically, this means waters on the Atlantic and the Pacific coasts, or more specifically, waters such as the Lower Columbia River between Washington and Oregon, Washington's Skagit and Willapa bays, and the famed Chesapeake Bay shared by Maryland and Virginia, as well as the countless tidal marshes and sloughs in the Carolinas, Florida,

The Columbia River estuary, a perfect example of productive duck water that moves in and out with the tides.

Vancouver Lake in southwestern Washington, a tidally influenced inland lake connected to the Columbia River via Deep River, is a waterfowl magnet.

This warm-water slough along Colorado's Front Range never freezes, and provides excellent gunning even when the nearby South Platte River is locked up tight.

hardy species such as mallards, black ducks, green-wing teal, and many of the divers, these late-season open water pockets serve as a last bastion, a final resting and loafing place before the inevitability of migration hits home. For some birds, as long as there is both open water and food available, the long trek southward is just some sort of instinctual memory yet to have been experienced.

A second point about moving water and its attractiveness to waterfowl lies in the fact that not all the sections of any flow move at the same rate or velocity. Look at any river, large or small, and chances are very good that you'll see a series of riffles and pools, each having its own current and current speed. Furthermore, each series of riffles and pools will likely feature elements such as eddies, backwaters, sharp bends, and oxbows, all of which offer decreased current conditions, with some showing little more movement than a small pond or lake – which, for all intents and purposes, these backwaters and eddies are. Furthermore, eddies, those slowly swirling changes of current direction so familiar to anglers, will often work to concentrate food such as floating acorns, vegetation, small fish – okay, so that's not so good – and mussels. These aquatic banquets then serve to attract ducks and, eventually, duck hunters.

Where the birds are

When progressing to variable number two, scouting, it's very important to remember that ducks use specific sections of moving water bodies for specific reasons. Many will be the times when a river or tidal bay will present two seemingly identical situations, the difference being that while one is constantly alive with duck activity, the second shows little or no action. On rivers or streams, this condition is relatively easy to identify and interpret, thanks to the more often than not obvious current. Waterfowl, like fish and people, don't enjoy fighting a current any more than necessary, and just like a trout or smallmouth will take up a position in a current seam or behind a large boulder that minimizes the flow, so, too, will waterfowl gravitate toward areas of decreased current. In rivers and streams, this means shallow pools, backwaters, or the downstream inside corner of any bend or turn in the river's course, all of which present possible locations for the placement of a permanent blind, or at the very least areas to be approached cautiously for those floating or walking the banks.

With tidal situations, waterfowlers need to remember that ducks will naturally fly along the front of the incoming water on the flow portion of the tide. Too, higher tides, the coming of which can be learned by the use of tide tables, mean that water will likely inundate shoreline grasses and other forage to a greater extent, and this condition will often result in greater numbers of birds leaving

Mississippi, Alabama, Louisiana, and Texas. Different in as much as where rivers flow horizontally, tidal areas "flow" in a vertical fashion, and in doing so present an entirely unique set of waterfowl hunting conditions, conditions which can be both very rewarding as well as very frustrating. Twice each day, these tidal waters ebb, or rush back to the ocean, and flow, or rise, and come inland. Surprising to some, many species of puddle ducks normally associated with fresh water or interior wetlands, species such as pintails, widgeon, and green-wing teal, also are home on coastal or tidal waters. Here, these birds follow the flow or edge of the tide each day, taking advantage of the new grasses and feeding locations which the incoming waters made available and accessible. And while tidal flows certainly can't be considered traditional in terms of moving waters to those living their lives in the interior of the Lower 48, those on the coasts, on the other hand, know these twice-daily fluctuations can provide as fast-paced and exciting a waterfowling opportunity as can be found on any river or stream. Or at times, anywhere.

The lure of moving water

What is it about moving water that birds find so attractive? In some cases, it's the fact that waters with current, and often any type or degree of current will suffice, are among the last waters to freeze during the winter. To

On moving water, the secret to success is location, location, location.

offshore loafing and roosting areas and coming inland to take advantage of this twice daily bonanza.

Birds and boats

Most moving waters offer waterfowlers a variety of possible hunting methods; however, the three most popular are floating, which includes the use of boat blinds, shooting from permanent blinds, and jump shooting.

In most cases, float trips involve a Point A to Point B style of journey; however some, such as the second-day hunt that Hassman and I enjoyed, can be made logistically simpler by the fact that the return portion of the trip involved little more than a short paddle upstream. Regardless of whether the trip is one-way or round-trip, one of the most important keys to float-hunting success is to have a plan. And when I say 'plan,' I mean more than just a 'We're going to go from here to there and shoot ducks....we hope' type of strategy.

Prior to our inaugural trip down the Mahoning that November, Hassman and I had planned to stop at various points along the way. Here we'd throw out a small spread, cover the canoe, and wait for an hour or so. Our thought was that this tactic would not only offer us the opportunity to enjoy gunning birds over the blocks and add to our bag, but it would also provide us the chance to spend time scouting and observing bird movement up and down the river. With this in mind, we included in our gear a small bag of mallard decoys and a 20-foot sec-

tion of camouflage burlap, thus creating the ultimate, not to mention very portable, blind and spread in a box. Always the Type A personality, I had gone so far as to pre-pick stopping points along the path of the river and marking them on my copy of the *Ohio Atlas & Gazetteer*; however, reality, as it often does, quickly set in and we simply let the birds decide where and when we'd stop and set up.

Planning can also take the form of deciding what particular section of a river to hunt. Some, like the Mahoning below Lake Milton, offer few choices; others, however, such as any one of the several tributary streams to the Columbia River found in the southwest corner of Washington – the Lewis, Kalama, Cowlitz, or Chehalis rivers for example – can present several different and similarly productive options. In the case of multiple options, it's often wise to spend an evening or two before the hunt driving as close to the course of the river as possible, stopping at likely looking locations along the way in order to see just what that particular section provides in terms of bird activity. Too, you should be on the lookout for what I'll call attractants – things such as agricultural ground in close proximity to the river, or better yet, close to natural resting waters such as a calm pool, eddy, or backwater. Birds feeding on harvested shoreline crops such as corn or peas will often afterwards make short hops back to the closest water available for a drink and a splash. Such places make excellent stopping points for the float hunter, but they can only be unveiled through

Fifteen feet of camouflage burlap and a dozen decoys turned this float trip into a watch and wait. This wait, as evidenced on the bow, wasn't long.

scouting, observation, and, yes, planning.

Although discussed in greater detail in the chapter on duck boats, I'd just like to take this chance to say that specialized boats are not – repeat: are not – necessary for float-hunting. Safe boats, yes. Camouflaged boats, maybe. But not special boats. Over the course of the past century, this country's rivers have been travelled and the passengers and crew have hunted waterfowl from rubber and wooden rafts to double-decked sternwheelers, and all in between. Now that's not saying that I would recommend the Mississippi be gunned from a paddlewheeler nor the Ohio from an innertube; however, I am saying that if it's safe, maneuverable, quiet, and in some cases can be hidden, then the skiff in question has all the potential in the world of being or becoming a duck boat. Ultimately, the water being hunted will dictate the boat used, and whether or not that craft is festooned with the latest in fashionable camouflage material, draped with willows and cattails, or simply painted in a random, Woodland-esque manner. Here, the best advice, and forgive me, please, is to go with the flow.

Water and safety go hand-in-hand. And the addition of firearms, heavy clothing, and extreme weather conditions and water temperatures simply compounds this situation. For these reasons, there are a handful of precautions that you can take to ensure that each and every float trip is a successful one, where here success translates into coming home alive.

First, always make it a point to file a float plan. This is nothing more than an itinerary that lists the date and place of the hunt, vehicle location, estimated time of return, and any other pertinent information. Leave this list with a wife, husband, friend, or family member – essentially, anyone that you would trust to worry if it got long around 10 PM and you weren't home yet. As the hunter, it's then your responsibility to contact the individual in charge of the float plan upon your return so they can stop worrying.

The second point concerns safety equipment. While several pieces of safety equipment are required by law and make very good sense, things such as fire extinguishers, orange signalling flags, and the like, there are other items – a cell phone, for instance – that might not be such a bad idea to include in your field gear. Other items could include a pair of disposable lighters, chemical handwarmers, energy bars, a lightweight survival blanket, small flashlight WITH good batteries, and a bare-bones first aid kit. While it sounds like a lot of gear, especially in a canoe, all of these items can fit into a pack smaller than a cigar box, and all can save your life should the situation arise.

And finally, there's that one indispensable item that we all are from time to time guilty of lacking – common sense. There's not a mallard hatched that's worth two men in a 17-foot canoe in three-foot seas, nor a sprig alive payment for a late-night telephone call to a loved one from the local sheriff's department. Simply put, water is the single most unforgiving element known to human kind. It shows no remorse, no pain, no joy. In its cruelest form, it takes all and gives nothing. There's always another, calmer day, when the waves aren't as high and the wind not as strong. Here, a little common sense goes a long way. It's like our dear friend, Ed Iman, a long-time salmon and walleye guide once said in reference to his home waters, the legendary Columbia River.

"She can be an awful mean bitch. There's days when I'd float her in a canoe. And then there's days when the Queen Mary's not big enough. It's all about respect."

Sitting and walking

But floating is not the only method for hunting the current. Some moving waters lend themselves well to the use of permanent blinds. The secret when gunning from permanent blinds is in-depth scouting. Often, such blinds are built along backwaters or sloughs, or at times on bends, pools, or riffles traditionally favored by both local and migrating birds. As many rivers support only a limited number of such traditional hotspots, these premier blind locations are often jealously guarded, or in many cases are handed down from generation to generation.

Jump shooting is another effective method for hunting moving waters. Similar to those gunning from permanent blinds, jump shooters can often take advantage of the birds' tendency to feed or loaf in specific sections of the river with regularity, and can concentrate their efforts on these more productive areas while bypassing the less productive stretches. One tactic used successfully by jump shooters across the country is to glass a section of river using binoculars. Once birds have been spotted, a stalk can be planned, thus eliminating the so-called "surprise factor" so common among meetings between jump shooters and waterfowl.

Decoys and moving water

Using decoys in moving waters can often rank right up there with trying to separate two cheap paper plates in terms of frustration. Every year, waterfowlers across the country lose dozens of decoys when hardware breaks, knots come untied – basically, when a few simple rules and guidelines aren't followed. True, decoys aren't nearly as costly as a good duck boat or that new Beretta; still, there's no need replacing that which doesn't need replacing.

Moving water and current means more drag on decoys and decoy lines. Therefore, lines should be strong and of the best quality, and knots, whether tied static to the decoy keel or to hardware such as a swivel which is then fastened to the decoy, should be likewise as strong. The knots I use depend upon the type of decoy cord I'm

Small creeks and streams like the one this fowler and his dog watch provide countless hours of fantastic gunning from coast to coast.

using. With nylon cord, a good, old-fashioned improved clinch knot, the same knot I use when I'm fishing, holds well, and as my father is fond of saying, "does nothing but get tighter the more you pull on it." With the popular Tangle-Free cords, however, I'll use a circular lead crimp-lock to ensure the cord doesn't pull free. An alternative to using the crimp-locks with the Tangle-Free cord is to double the cord and pass it through the "eye" of the decoy keel. The loop is then pulled entirely over the decoy and pulled snug. A half-hitch is then tied in the tag end of the cord to prevent the tag end from pulling through, and the excess clipped off. It's quick, easy, and holds surprisingly well.

Here's a trick that I use when working with decoys in current. Approximately 3 inches back from the eye on the decoy keel, drill a ⅛-¼ inch hole (water keel). Or, if using weighted keels, heat the tips of an ordinary fence staple with a propane torch and push the staple into the keel, again approximately 3 inches behind the eye. Tying the decoy off to this modified eye makes the decoy "swim" back and forth, with the lengthened leading edge of the keel acting like the lip on a crankbait. Typically, I'll use three or four of these modified decoys per dozen.

Tidal situations spell an entirely different set of conditions for the decoy user. As tide waters rise, decoy cords that were fine at a foot in length become stretched to their limit. Eventually, the cork which is the decoy lifts both cord and weight from the bottom, leaving the

Tip – To make your river decoys 'swim' more realistically, tie the anchor cord to a point three or four inches back from the leading edge of the keel.

decoy to float about on its own, and, depending upon the wind and where you're hunting, either out to Europe or China, whichever's closer. These rising waters, too, mean that decoys must be moved constantly either in or out, depending upon whether you're hunting the ebb or flow. To remedy this, at least in part, it's easy to rig several decoys, six to a dozen is common, on one main line with weights at both ends, or, in calm conditions, with a single anchor. Decoys rigged as such can be easily moved in or out as the tide dictates.

Decoys: Fakes
and Frauds

A western Washington sunrise over a small mixed decoy spread. It's time.

Any activity in which you use more than one of any particular item lends itself to controversy. This is especially true of duck decoys.

Try this. Go into your local small town Minute Mart or café. Go at noon, so that all the farmers and bankers, church hierarchy and retired townfolk are there eating the Swiss Steak special, complete with oven browns and a fountain Pepsi, for $2.99

Now, stand in the middle of the room, cross your arms in a relaxed pose, and stare at a point in the corner where the floor meets the wall. Before long, one of the bib-clad corn growers is going to wander over. He may

This young waterfowler will likely never grow out of his fascination with decoys and the art that is decoying ducks. *Photo courtesy of Mossy Oak.*

not say much, if anything, but he'll look to see what you're looking at. Three or four more patrons, all out at lunch time to pick up a pack of Camels and top off their fuel tanks, will take a second or two to throw a look your way. A couple will step a little closer, bend at the waist, and peer intently into the corner before wandering off. One of those folks will actually come back in after leaving to see if you're still there and to try to figure out just what in the hell you're looking at.

That, in a nutshell, is how decoys work. It's a fake duck – you – trying to attract the attention of at least one real duck – the farmer – while hopefully garnering a passing glance from some others – the smokers. The inquisitive guy who came back through the door of the shop for a second look would be a bonus. Kind of like a bunch of blue-wing teal that for whatever reason insist on swinging the blind just one more time mere seconds after having been shot at. Really, it's no more involved than that. Duck hunters just make it appear so.

A (very) brief history

Decoys in some shape or form have been around and in use ever since humans decided that wild birds and animals were good things to eat. Early Native Americans, for instance, were known to drape themselves with the hides of previously fallen deer and buffalo, a tactic which allowed them to approach their prey much more closely

and to within range of their primitive bows and spears. Some would argue that such a technique might be considered more ancient camouflage than true decoy use; however, the basic decoy premise, getting close to game by presenting the illusion of a similar species in a natural, relaxed environment, certainly can't be denied. These same peoples are often credited with devising and using the first known waterfowl decoys. Some of these earliest decoys were little more than duck-shaped piles of mud or vegetation placed at the edge of a pond, lake, or other wetland area. Over time, these mud-ducks gave way to more realistic versions such as actual preserved waterfowl skins, which were stretched over small clumps of grass or brush. Later, these same skins would be filled with soft, pliable materials such as grass or moss and sewn shut, a revolutionary process which resulted in not only the birth of the modern duck decoy, but the school of taxidermy as well.

With the invention of black and then smokeless powders, along with the design and evolution of shoulder-fired arms, waterfowl decoys began to step out of the shadows and more into the spotlight. Important to note, also, would be the increase in popularity of wildfowl as a culinary experience, particularly along the then booming and population – swelling Atlantic Coast. With this rise in the nation's interest in wild duck dinners came a corresponding growth in the number of men willing and very able to supply the country's finest restaurants with their much-requested avian guest of honor. Thus was created the market hunter, a breed to whom can be attributed, at least in part, the evolution of decoys, *and* the institution of wildlife regulations, hunting seasons, and bag limits.

At this early stage, the vast majority of the country's duck and goose decoys were fashioned from wood, and were in every sense of the word works of art. Entire spreads of pintails, canvasbacks, redheads, and bluebills – all birds of the Atlantic Flyway and all species known, some too well, to the market gunners who called the Eastern Seaboard home – rode the waters of Cheasapeake Bay and a thousand hidden saltwater marshes and nearshore inland ponds. Other species such as swans, then legal game in most of United States, and black ducks, another Atlantic favorite, as well as a long list of shorebirds including Wilson's snipe, plovers, and yellowlegs, all of which could be at any time part of the wingshooter's daily bag, were also brought to life though in wooden form, and all used at one time or another as wooden accomplices in the waterfowler's activities.

Although wood was by far the most commonly used material for making decoys during these early years, other materials such as cork and, surprisingly enough, lead and iron, were also used. Relatively easy to work with, cork afforded hunters and carvers a lightweight yet durable alternative to wood. Metal decoys, while making little sense in terms of field use due to their weight, were crafted and called upon to serve as psuedo-anchors by those hunters gunning from sink boxes, a very popular and devastatingly effective – so much so that their use has been prohibited for years in the United States - means of concealing oneself literally below the surface of the water. Because of their elevation, or lack thereof, sink boxes were prone to filling with water, often as a result of wave action. To combat this, hunters would place wings or aprons, little more than glorified pieces of snow fence or fence-like slatting, leading out from the four sides of the box. The metal decoys were then placed on the wings in order to both hold the wings down and the blind itself in place. The fact that they were shaped like ducks and geese certainly did no harm to the overall appearance of the blind and decoy spread.

Today, most waterfowl decoys are made of plastic. Incredibly easy and inexpensive to manufacture, thanks to an abundance of raw material and to technological advancements such as injection molding, plastic decoys provide the ultimate in weight reduction, realism, and durability – all at a price that allows most hunters to assemble spreads of dozens, if not hundreds, of decoys, and of many different species. And while there's much to be said for the benefits of these plastic decoys, their entry into the waterfowler's world displaced a piece of hunting tradition the likes of which few see, let alone use, today – the decoy as a hand-crafted and very effective work of art.

Decoys in detail

For the waterfowler looking to take his first steps into the world known as decoy acquisition, a practice that like the purchase of both firearms and fishing lures has a beginning but no visible end, there's really not a whole lot of choices out there. At least not in terms of style.

Essentially, duck decoys come in three variations. There's the traditional or full-bodied version, the half-shell, and the silhouette. The heaviest and most cumbersome to carry, particularly when the transportation process involves a bag toted on one's shoulders, the traditional full-bodied water decoys comprise probably 95 percent of the decoys currently in use.

Typically, full-bodied decoys are available in three sizes; essentially, small (standard), medium (magnum), and large (super magnum). Standard decoys will be very close in size to the real thing, while magnum and super magnum blocks, a old-time nickname given to decoys back in the days when they were made from blocks of wood and a phrase that's still relatively common today, will often be two, three, or even four times the size of a live duck. Magnum and super magnum decoys are often used in big-water types of situations, where their large size makes them very visible, even from long distances.

Lightweight, water keel decoys like the hen mallard the author is placing are the perfect choice for the walk-in freelancer.

Hunters gunning over smaller waters, too, can benefit from these larger decoys, as fewer blocks can often be used *and* can be just as effective as a bigger spread – a definite plus, again, when a decoy spread must be carried in rather than trucked in.

One characteristic that all water decoys, with the exception of a handful of specialty decoys to be discussed later, share is a keel. This keel, often nothing more than a plastic protrusion running the length of the decoy from head to tail, serves both to help keep the decoy upright, particularly under windy conditions, as well as to ensure that the block tracks true, or in a straight line; again, a variable influenced by wind and in some cases, current.

Two types of keels, at least in the case of plastic decoys, exist today. These are the water keel, and the weighted keel. Hollow throughout, water keels fill with water – hence the name – and rely on this introduced weight for ballast, ballast which prevents the decoy from tipping over. Water keel decoys are light, and make an excellent choice for walk-in hunters prone to strapping decoys and decoy bags on their backs. On the downside, water keel decoys may not work as well as a heavier decoy under windy or wavy conditions, and often show a tendency to ski or slice on their anchor cord. In other words, they lie on their sides, a trait that few real live mallards or pintails ever exhibit in the wild.

Weighted keel decoys, on the other hand, will stand up much better to wind and waves than will their lighter

Carefully wrapping each block at day's end helps keep decoy bag tangles to a minimum.

A Feather Flex original RTU (Ready to Use) decoy showing anchor cord, weight, and depth locking system.

counterparts, and often make an excellent choice for those hunting big water, heavy current, or under very windy conditions; however, because of the additional weight – commonly sand is used to fill the keels before the blocks leave the factory – weighted keel decoys can pose a problem for those without a means of transporting the blocks, a means, that is, other than on their backs.

Like most choices regarding outdoor gear, the decision to purchase and use water keels versus weighted keel decoys is often one of personal preference and usage. Some hunters will buy a dozen or two of each, using the water keels for their small water walk-in hunts, and the weighted keels for more open water outings, perhaps when a boat is available for transporting both hunters and gear.

Two other basic types of duck decoys are available, each with a variation or two. These are the half-shell, and the silhouette. Half-shells look just as the name implies, and are basically the upper half of a duck. Half-shells are commonly used in field or dry land situations, although several companies today market half-shells called convertibles which incorporate a unique concave keel that allows the decoy to be used either on land or in the water. Lightweight and stackable one inside the next, half-shells lend themselves well in situations where large numbers of decoys are called for, particularly when those decoys must be carried in by hand. Often, half-shells, as well as silhouettes, are used to supplement spreads of tradition-

al full-bodied decoys, a tactic that can work very well, particularly late in the season.

Silhouettes are another tool in the waterfowler's decoy arsenal. The lightest and most easily transported – not to mention stored – of the decoys, silhouettes are little more than a two-dimensional cut-out painted to look like either a duck or goose. A stake, often shaped or painted to serve as the decoy's "leg," is simply stuck into the ground, making these types of decoys one of the easiest and least time-consuming to use, and in large numbers. At one time rather primitive and duck-like only in the vaguest sense of the word, silhouette decoys have evolved to where today, companies such as Outlaw Decoys and Flambeau are producing two-dimensional versions complete with photographic images that look as real as any duck or goose alive.

The best advice for the newcomer just getting into the decoy-buying game is to make sure you do your homework, and research all of your choices well before buying. Decoys are available from a wide variety of sources, including local retailers, large outdoor chains such as Gander Mountain, Bass Pro, and Cabela's, and mail-order houses, as well as from any number of suppliers currently working the Internet. Prices can and often do vary, sometimes greatly, from company to company and from manufacturer to manufacturer, and it makes good sense to shop around a bit before buying. Remember, though, that quality decoys should last a lifetime, even with reasonably heavy use; however, the key word here is "quality."

Riggings and weights

Jeff Johnson, an avid waterfowler who makes his home in eastern Iowa, tells the story of three young hunters making what he could only guess was their first excursion into the world of the waterfowler.

Following a very productive morning's hunt on a local marsh, Johnson and a gunning companion were headed back to the boat ramp. On their way, they noticed three young men, all of whom are wearing somewhat disgruntled and frustrated expressions. Johnson com-

Decoy weights like these from Hunter's Specialties come in a wide variety of shapes and sizes.

When used on shallow inland marshes, puddle duck decoys can be simply rigged with a short section of anchor cord and a light six-ounce weight.

mented to his partner that while they had enjoyed a nice shoot not 400 yards away from the threesome, he couldn't recall having heard the young men ever fire a shot.

As is customary when hunters' paths cross in the field, Johnson greets the young men with the usual – "How you doing? Having any luck?"

"Not a thing," says the apparent ringleader of the group. "Haven't had anything even come close. And besides, we've spent most of the morning chasing these decoys. 'Bout the time we get 'em set right, the wind starts to blow them all over the place. Don't know what to do about that," he complained.

A helpful and considerate sort, Johnson offered up his own brand of advice. "Are you sure your decoy cords are long enough? Are the knots tight? How about your anchors? Are the anchors holding well in this bottom?" Typical questions, or so he thought.

It was then that the group leader, now with an embarrassed and borderline horrified look on his face, said, almost too softly to hear, "You mean they're supposed to have cords and anchors on them?"

Johnson swears the story is true. Surprisingly odd, even for a group of novices, but true nonetheless.

With the exception of a handful of specialty riggings, preparing decoys – and here we're talking about water-use, floating blocks – for the field isn't, as champion duck caller, Buck Gardner, is fond of saying, rocket science. Essentially, it's nothing more than tying one end of a piece of string to the decoy and the other to something heavy enough to prevent the decoy from floating away. Period. Still, as duck hunters, we put a lot of effort into making the simple complicated, or at least more involved, and such is the case with decoy riggings.

Basically, decoy riggings come in two parts. The first is the anchor cord; the second is the anchor itself. In the past, any of 1,000 different things have been used, both for anchors and anchor cord, ranging from but not limited to binder twine, kite string, shoe laces, spark plugs, large nuts and bolts, bricks, and yes, even rocks. And with the exception of bricks, which can have a place in deep-water gang rig applications – we'll get into that later – there certainly are better and more efficient, not to

mention more esthetically pleasing, alternatives to these age-old favorites.

Today, decoy cord comes in two basic categories – nylon twine or cord, and synthetic (plastic). Nylon twine is probably the most commonly used, partially because it works well, and in part because it's cheap. Nylon holds a knot very well, resists molding and rotting, and comes in a variety of colors, one of which will surely match any sort of bottom type including sand, mud, grass, or rock. Plastics, on the other hand, such as the original Tangle-Free decoy cord or Hunter's Specialties' Tangle-Proof version, provide a no-mess, no-fuss alternative to the traditional nylon; however, folks will have to decide for themselves whether the name follows through in terms of effectiveness and benefit. Some hunters, myself included, find the plastics hard to work with, especially in cold weather, don't hold knots well – separate crimps and knot locks are available and advised when using these plastic cords – and stretch the definition of no-tangles to the limit; however, they're nonetheless very popular all across the country, so someone must not be having a problem.

Like decoy cord, decoy anchors come in different designs, each of which is intended to make life easier for the waterfowler. The most basic of these designs is nothing more than a lead weight, something very similar to the well-known bank or bell fishing sinker. In some cases, this bell shape gives way to what's known as a mushroom weight. This mushroom design provides the

Paying attention to decoy details – anchor and cord organization for one – will pay off in aces when it comes time to use those particular blocks again.

ultimate in holding power in many types of bottoms, including sand and mud, and under even the harshest wind and wave conditions. Both the bell weights and mushroom weights are typically available in four to eight ounce versions.

Unlike the bell or mushroom weights which simply hang from or must be wrapped, along with a foot or so of their cord, around the neck of the decoy, there are weights available which eliminate much of the frustration and cursing normally associated with tangled masses of decoys and string. Some of the oldest and most traditional of these weights come in the shape of thin donuts or ovals, and are simply slipped over the head of the decoy when not in use. Another version, and one which rivals the mushroom design in terms of holding power, features a small lead cup and accompanying heavy-duty rubber band. At the end of the day, the cup is placed over the decoy's bill, and the rubber band slipped around the back of the decoy's head, holding it in place.

Modern weights have taken this ease and convenience one step further. Today, strap-style weights, long lead straps or pencil-shaped weights which end in a mushroom head, allow the anchors themselves to be wrapped around the decoy's neck, or in some cases, around a portion of the keel. Convenient and very painless, yes, but if these designs were to have one fault, it would be that the repeated bending and straightening of the wrapping process can quickly crack or stress the soft

lead resulting in a very shortened lifespan for the original anchor. True, such broken weights can easily be bent and hooked together, thus giving them several additional seasons afield, but then, you're right back to square one.

Still, who's to say that spark plugs won't work? After all, they do make great – and very cheap – shore-fishing sinkers.

Specialty blocks and bags

Into every life, some specialty "stuff," psuedo-fancy things that we just can't live without, must fall. And the duck hunter's life is certainly no exceptions. Face it, if it weren't for gadgets, waterfowlers would be afield with little more than a single-shot shotgun and a dozen water-keel decoys.

Still, there's without question an art to making a decoy spread come alive. It does take skill to transform 24 plastic ducks into a living, breathing, moving, wave-making flock of hungry, "hey, there's no reason for you up there not to visit us down here" mallards. Enter the specialty decoys.

Specialty decoys, for lack of a better phrase, are those non-traditional decoys that help bring life to a spread. Remember those words – bring life. If you watch any group of ducks on the water, you'll soon see that there's a common denominator regardless of where you're watching or what kind of birds you're looking at. And that common denominator is natural movement. While some birds are tipping up in search of food, others are preening. Still others are nestled on the leeward side of the pond sleeping. Every now and then, one of the birds will rise up and stretch his wings. All the while, birds will be coming and going, kind of like the New York subway at rush hour. There's a constant flow around the pond, and that flow is what you're trying to achieve in your decoy spread.

Sleeping and preening decoys, both of which are currently available, help lend an air of relaxation and naturalism to the spread as a whole. So, too, do tip-up decoys, otherwise known as feeders or duck butts. These unique half-blocks feature the back end of a duck, and are just one way to transmit an "all's clear, food here" signal to a passing flock of birds.

And while a natural appearance is certainly important, nothing is more important or vital to the success of a decoy spread than is movement. Again going back to our ficitional flock of ducks, one of the things that you'll notice is that there's always some type of movement, whether that be birds flapping their wings, swimming, feeding, flying, or what have you. Important to note here, too, is that all the water-based movement, such as swimming and tipping up, produces ripples, waves, and

Some hunters separate their decoys by species or sex – note only the bull can blocks here. This practice can make set-up easier.

splashes – all "all's well" signs, and all vital parts of the whole decoy spread equation.

Fortunately, imparting movement to a decoy spread isn't all that difficult, nor does it have to be costly. One of the most inexpensive and most effective methods for creating movement within the spread is through a jerk cord. A jerk cord is nothing more than a long string attached at one end to a solid object, the other leading to the blind, and on which has been tied one or two light decoys. A couple quick yanks on the cord, and the decoys bounce and swim across the surface of the water, themselves looking alive while at the same time creating the waves and ripples that shout "feeding ducks here." A two-foot piece of surgical tubing or dark-colored bungee cord can be used between the decoys and the solid object to provide even more resistence and bounce. Another version uses a heavy anchor such as a brick – I used three, 10-ounce sturgeon fishing weights – and the aforementioned long cord. The cord is run through a brass snap swivel clipped to the anchor eye of a light water-keel decoy before being tied to the weight (brick). The tag end of the cord is then run to the blind. Again, a couple sharp jerks on the cord, and the decoy bounces like Dolly Parton on a mechanical bull.

But while jerk cords can be the cheapest way to impart movement into a decoy spread, they're certainly not the only method. Today, several companies produce specialized decoys designed to shake, quiver, wobble, vibrate, and any of a dozen different things, all of which can be very effective in terms of creating the illusion of ducks on the water and in motion. Wind power, too, can be harnessed and used to the waterfowler's advantage, thanks to specialty decoys such as wind socks, flags, and the well-known duck and goose magnets – all of which lend to this "flock in motion" vision.

One of the most controversial waterfowling subjects to come along in years is the recent popularity of the, and I'll use the name generically, Robo-duck decoy. These mechanical, battery-powered decoys use small motors (although wind can and is often substituted given the proper conditions) to turn a metal shaft upon which is fastened a pair of wing-like appendages. Dark on one side, light on the other, these wings spin at a high rate of speed, often at from 250 to 350 revolutions per minute, producing what's often referred to as a strobe-like effect. In reality, the flashing of the dark/light patterns are intended to simulate the on-off flicker of a duck's wings as it lands. Those who have used such mechanical decoys have for the most part been awestruck by the effectiveness of this latest waterfowling gadget; thus the controversy as to whether or not the decoys are "too effective," and might have a negative impact on water-fowl populations due to higher harvests nationwide. Some states, it's said, are looking into the possibility of prohibiting the use of such mechanical devices; howev-er, at this point, it remains a wait-and-see proposition.

One last decoy that I'd feel remiss if I were to not mention is the confidence decoy. Here again like natural

The Robo-Duck. Some hate it; some love it. It's your decision.

It pays to purchase the best quality decoy bags available. There's nothing more frustrating than bags that rip, or worse, dump decoys along the way.

or motion decoys, confidence decoys simply add to the overall "wild" appearance of the spread. Typically, confidence decoys are not of a waterfowl species, but rather of a water or land bird known to associate with waterfowl. The most commonly seen confidence decoy is the great blue heron, a wise bird with tremendous eyesight and whose presence is a comfort to birds undecided as to the true nature of the gathering below. Other confidence decoys include American coots, sea gulls, and crows.

On the subject of decoy bags. Decoy bags serve two primary purposes. The first of these is storage, both during the season as well as during the off-season. The second involves the actual transportation of the decoy from Point A, typically known as the house, to Point B, referred to in most circles as the hunting site.

For those looking at decoy bags as little more than a storage bin, the vital statistics of the bag itself, other than size, is of little importance; however, for those who view these bags as steroid-ridden knapsacks, there's a bit more to the decision as to which to buy – and which to get someone else to carry.

Field bags, those bags actually filled with decoys and carried into the field on your back, should be (1) well-made, as the duck swamp is no place to be doing rough surgery on a decoy bag, and (2) as comfortable as something used for this purpose and shaped as such can be. Comfort, where decoy bags are concerned, is often a fleeting if not unobtainable thing; however, bags that fit or that can be adjusted to fit snugly by a series of straps and clips, and padding, can both contribute greatly to the ease by which the blocks are packed into the field. Like decoys, decoy bags, especially those that are going to be used for carrying blocks in and out of the field, should be researched and even tested before being purchased.

Oh, and one last thing. A seat cushion, like the Bunsaver by Hunter's Specialties or something similar, worn over the kidney area and between the decoy bag and your back will make all the difference in the world, and save you from those painful pokes and prods that come courtesy of plastic bills and pintail sprigs.

10
Over the Blocks

Decoy Spreads: The Basics

Countless articles and, yes, even entire books, have been written and devoted to the intricacies, nay, the science, of arranging decoys. And while it's certainly true that a good decoy spread will, particularly under certain conditions such as weather and hunting pressure, outperform a poor decoy spread, the Type A-personality method of decoy arrangement actually takes the process a little beyond what it need be.

Still, for those who would immediately disagree with any comment even alluding to the fact that decoy arrangement isn't a paramount consideration, let me quickly add that, yes, decoy placement can be important. Fortunately, there are a handful of fast and easy guidelines for any waterfowler still stymied by decoys and how they should be arranged.

1. **The decoys themselves.** Like most trinkets in the realm of the hunter, decoys are designed with two things in mind. First, catch the hunter; second, catch the ducks. Fancy packaging and new-wave accessories like self-winding anchor lines and other hang-on items mean little when it comes right down to true test of any waterfowl decoy – does it work, and work consistently? Better said, it's what lies inside the box that's important to the success of any duck hunting venture. Not the pretty picture on the outside. That said, my suggestion here is to take a good, hard look at the decoys themselves. Are they lifelike? Are there details enough to make them look realistic? And what about the paint? In years past, I've seen some fantastic-looking blocks ruined simply by the manufacturer, or in some cases the original owner, using the wrong colors. And sometimes in the wrong places. The bottom line here? Get the most realistic, natural-looking decoys in your price range.

Picking up at the end of the day. Four hands always makes it easier.

On small waters, such as this western Washington puddle, it's often best to downsize the entire rig.

2. **Natural.** The plain and simple truth behind decoy spreads is natural. Forget most of what you've read and begin to think naturally. Or think like a duck. And to think like a duck, it's best if you know as much as you possibly can about ducks. Ducks at rest and feeding, for instance, are most often arranged in loose groups, typically with ample spacing between each bird or pair of birds. Some birds might be sleeping or preening, while others are tipping up in the shallow or just generally gin-wacking around. That's all ducks really have to do all day. Because of these lolly-gagging habits, I subscribe to what I call the "random placement theory of decoy arrangement." All this means is that more often than not, my decoy spreading process consists of little more than me standing in a central location, a point which later becomes the "hole" or landing area, and tossing the blocks to the four corners at random. Certainly, I take the wind into consideration, particularly on larger bodies of water where the birds have more airspace over the decoys to work with; however, this haphazard approach to decoy placement seems to work well under most conditions.

Conversely, ducks that are alarmed for whatever reason will be tightly packed or grouped, with heads raised. These birds are listening. They're alert and edgy. Such a situation doesn't say, "Hey, come on over here. Everything's all right" to passing flocks. Essentially, the more you know and understand about waterfowl biology – and this can mean nothing more than watching the birds on the pond outside the office window or around the lake at the nearby city park – the more prepared you'll be to duplicate or replicate what you've seen in the field. Naturally.

3. **Put the decoys where the birds can see them.** Sounds simple, but some folks, for whatever reason, insist on hiding their blocks. Take the pair of hunters I encountered on a flooded field along the Scioto River south of Columbus, Ohio, one morning. As I watched, flight after flight of late-season mallards and blacks streamed overhead their blind, oblivious to the two dozen plastic ducks below. Why? Part of the reason – and I say part because the calling or the unreasonable facsimile thereof might have contributed to their lack of success – was that instead of arranging the decoys in and around the small puddles of open, non-vegetated water, the duo had opted to put each of their blocks next to, or in some cases actually inside, the hundreds of clumps of fallen goldenrod, foxtail, and sawgrass. After half an hour, I couldn't stand it any longer and I walked down to introduce myself. Not surprising, the blind held two young men, both of whom were enjoying the day afield after having learned that school had been cancelled due to snow. Who said duck hunters were smart when it came to weather conditions? The boys

This northeastern Ohio beaver swamp called for only a dozen standard floaters – as natural a setup as can be made. And light, too.

A beautiful and very natural spread of Flambeau blocks being put to use on a small marsh. Note the distance between decoys, spacing which says 'nothing at all wrong down here.'

Used in conjunction with traditional blocks, silhouette decoys can enhance a setup by increasing the visibility of the entire spread.

seemed nice, so I offered a couple suggestions in terms of decoy arrangement. Twenty minutes, a couple soft quacks, and a feeding chuckle later, the older of the pair was wading back to the blind with a beautiful drake mallard, one of a dozen birds that committed to the boys' now-visible spread like it had been arranged around the last remaining water on the planet. Had it not been for a bad case of accuracy trauma, the tally would have been greater. Still, the lesson here was simple. If you're not going to put the decoys where the birds can see them, you're better off leaving the entire spread in the garage.

4. **Wind direction.** The relationship of wind direction and decoy arrangment goes back to an understanding of waterfowl biology. Or more precisely, of aeronautics. Waterfowl, like airplanes, prefer to both take off and land into the wind. I say prefer because the birds can actually perform either act in any of a million different directions regardless of the wind at the time; however, they'd rather have the wind in their favor. Particularly when landing. Because of this tendency, and the fact that ducks typically don't fly low over sitting birds but would rather land behind or to one side, a trait that I can only attribute to their paranoia of a colleague suddenly jumping into the air and thus creating all the elements necessary for a mid-air collision, the placement or location of the main body of the decoy spread as it relates to the blind is

dependent almost totally on wind direction. Now that you're confused, let me simplify the process. Imagine a huge clock. Your blind – and a fine blind it is – is located in the center of the face at the point where the hands connect. The number 12 is north, three east, six south, and nine west. The rule regarding decoys and blinds is then "same time, same place." To define - if, for example, you have a due east (3 o'clock) wind, then your decoys are arranged in an approximately 3 o'clock position, give or take a few minutes. "If the wind's from the right," says The Duck Commander, Phil Robertson, "you put your decoys to the right. If the wind's from the left, put your decoys to the left." It's pretty simple. What you don't want is a wind that hits you in the face, as the birds will have a tendency to approach from behind your blind location as they turn and come into the breeze. At times that's all you have to work with, and you have to deal with it as best you can. A better alternative is to move your blind position, or your position in the blind if that's an option, through 180 degrees and put the wind at your back.

5. **The hole.** It's Christmas, and you're driving your brand new Ford Explorer around the Wal-Mart parking lot looking for some place safe to stow it for the next two hours. As is often the case around the holidays, people – translation: Everyone and his brother - have driven and been bussed to this par-

An on-the-water view of a natural looking decoy spread. Some movement on the water, however, would help.

Note the gap or "hole" between the two blobs of canvasback decoys. Birds will typically gravitate toward this safe landing area.

Surveying the set-up on the Mississippi – something all duck hunters do. And frequently.

ticular store, you're positive, from several states distant. Now the question. Would you feel more at ease parking in a location where you have three empty spots to the left and another four to the right, or one with only inches to spare between the 1976 Pinto and the 1969 Buick Electra 225 with the missing fender skirt and the remnants of what you can only assume is a raccoon tail flopping from the radio antenna? You want the space, don't you? Well, ducks do too. Thus, the hole. Technically, if such a word can be used here, the hole in a decoy spread is just that – a space, be it water or field, which is devoid of decoys and which provides an attractive and uncrowded landing zone within the whole of the decoy spread. The hole is essentially an unspoken invitation to "land, land right here." Size? Actually, the size of the hole depends upon the situation, or variables such as the size of the area being hunted and the number of decoys being used. Too small a hole and the birds might likely not feel comfortable landing in such a confined area. Often, birds landing outside the hole or at the fringes of the decoy spread can mean (a) the hole's too small, or (b) the decoy spread is too tight. The remedy here is to simply enlarge the landing area, and perhaps put a little more spacing between the individual blocks; however, care should be taken not to make the hole so large as to create potential landing areas outside your effective shooting range.

All this isn't to say that every bird that lands in or around the decoy spread is, without fail, going to light directly in the center of the hole you've created. It's not going to happen that way; still, "the hole" creates and increases the opportunity or possibility that it will happen.

6. **Funneling.** This aspect goes back both to the aforementioned creation of the hole or landing area, as well as to many of the decoy placement techniques and strategies that hunters around the country have heard tell of throughout the course of waterfowling history. These are the alphabetical or figure-form arrangements. These include the popular and oft-mentioned "C," "V," "X," and "J" patterns, as well as such favorites as the fish-hook and the teardrop. And while I have earlier admitted that I am a personal fan of the random placement theory of decoy placement, there's no doubt about the effectiveness of these patterns or offshoots – hybrids, variations, what-have-you – of these traditional spreads. But *why* are they effective? How do they work? Basically, despite their visual differences, each of these patterns share one common and very important denominator – the shape serves to funnel birds to the shooters. Period. But first and for those unfamiliar with these arrangements, a brief description of these very basic spreads –

Small boats, such as the AquaPod pictured here, can make decoy setup and retrieval a simple matter.

The C – The letter C. The rounded or back portion of the letter leads into the wind, while the pocket between the two "arms" creates the hole or landing zone. Blind location along the curve of the letter depends upon the wind direction.

The V – A rough-shaped 'V,' with the open portion perpendicular to the wind. Blind location is at the point. A duck/goose combination variation of this pattern uses a string of puddle duck decoys to form the upwind leg, the blind at the point, and a break in the opposite leg before placing six or eight Canada goose floaters in a ragged semi-circle at the tip of the other. Good big water rig.

The X – Often used by field hunters for ducks and geese. Rough X-shape, with the blind at the center. Provides multiple landing areas, making it a good choice for open-water or four/five-gun situations.

The J – Technically a mirror-image or backwards 'J' pattern. Leading edge or arm of the 'J' points downwind at a rough 45 degree angle to the blind. Curved portion or tail of the letter continues slightly upwind past the blind to create a pocket directly in front of the hide. Popular arrangement among diver duck fanatics as birds such as cans, redheads, and scaup all show a tendency to fly or cruise the outer edge of the elongated arm. Layout

hunters often position themselves right in the pocket in order to take advantage of this characteristic. Works well on puddlers, too. Also called the fish-hook pattern in some locales.

The Teardrop – a.k.a. The Blob. Teardrop or rough pyramidal shape leading upwind from the blind location. Favorite of snow goose hunters who capitalize on the species' greedy, "I want to feed first" nature. Good over water, particularly when augmented with a small spread of Canada goose floaters in effective range, but downwind of the blind.

All that description said, the discussion now turns to the original topic, funneling. Truth is, the concept behind funneling is as elemental as it sounds, for it's the art, or perhaps the magic, of directing or guiding birds through the use and strategic placement of decoys (1) into those areas where they should be, and (2) out of those areas where they shouldn't be. Certainly, the concept doesn't work as precisely as the explanation might suggest, nor does it work all the time; however, funneling is just one of the almost infinite number of tricks and tactics with which waterfowlers can arm themselves. Essentially, it's a case of better to have it and not use it than to need it and not have it.

In its purest form, funneling capitalizes on the hesitancy ducks have to both fly low over their waterbound colleagues and land in small, bird-crowded

Despite their proximity to shore, many of these decoys were rigged in 10 to 12 feet of water on this steep-sloped quarry pond. The land-based solution? Invisible monofilament fishing line tied to the anchors and used to retrieve each block.

widgeon. I've seen few of them in the wild. What I do see throughout the course of the waterfowling year are decoy spreads where the individual blocks are something out of a Salvador Dali painting.

I won't beleaguer the point here, that point being that the effectiveness of a decoy spread depends upon the effectiveness of each decoy as an individual unit. Thus, if those individuals aren't, well, attractive, then the entire spread suffers. In other words, the aesthetics of each and every decoy affects the overall performance of the spread. Translation? Keep 'em clean and well-maintained.

It's true that waterfowlers are often sticklers when it comes to maintaining decoy cords and anchors. After all, who wants $80 worth of plastic ducks floating downriver? That's a bad thing. And while it's certainly a good idea to annually inspect all of the cords and anchors within a spread, replacing or retying those where necessary, it's also important, though vastly overlooked, to maintain the overall appearance of the individual blocks throughout the course of the season. Remember #2 above – naturalism? Well, it should come as no surprise that decoys covered with mud, dirt, and debris aren't exactly what most would call natural.

Fortunately, periodic cleaning and maintenance is for the most part relatively easy. For instance, water-use decoys covered with duck weed or mud can be quickly rinsed off, either in the field through a short dunking or at home with the garden hose. It's a good idea to get into the habit of cleaning each decoy, or at the very least checking each block, at the end of the each hunting trip. This saves time and a great deal of effort at the start of the subsequent outings. Personally, I also use this cleaning time to inspect things such as knots and anchors. Do I do such an inspection every time? To be brutally honest, the answer is no; *but* I do check lines and weights at least once each season. And sometimes more often if any particular bag of decoys is seeing an extraordinary amount of field time.

Is all this work and worry – the strategizing, the cleaning, the wind – is it really just taking something as simple as the placement of plastic ducks and putting it right up there with the study of nuclear physics and microphyte communities? I don't think so. Remember, what you're doing when you use decoys is not only creating an illusion, but filling out or embodying the whole of that illusion. A decoy spread, essentially, is nothing more than an attactant, that eye-catching flick of a tail or split-second movement intended solely as an attention grabber. The trick then, once the attention has been gained, is to hold it long enough and deeply enough so as to draw that flock of mallards or gadwall from their original 500 yards to 35 yards or less. And this is where all the detail comes into play – the final 35 yards.

areas. For instance, the classic "J" or fish-hook pattern uses the downwind or longer leg of decoys almost as an invisible fence or pathway which the birds follow or are funneled by until such a time as they reach and can comfortably land in the open-water pocket provided by the crook or hook of the 'J.' By no coincidence, this open-water pocket is located within exceptional gunning range of the blind. This same principle applies to any alphabetically-designed decoy spread, regardless of whether it's the 'C,' 'X,' 'V,' or what have you. At the risk of giving waterfowl far too many human qualities, funneling merely creates a situation where the birds are provided the option of by-passing those areas of higher bird-to-bird competition (read: decoys) or of possible air traffic control issues (again read: decoys), and instead choosing that option (translation: landing zone) which limits or eliminates these variables.

Care and cleaning of plastic ducks

Honestly, I can't remember the last time I looked over a flock of what I would consider perfectly normal ducks and noticed that a vast majority of them were covered in mud and dirt, feathers askew with many missing. Drake mallards with Holstein-esque heads mottled lime-green and white. Oh, and moss-draped

Tip - When breaking ice for a spread, try to fracture large pieces and slide them under the remaining ice shelf. From the air, hundreds of little chunks look just like a mixed drink with ducks on it.

A day on the Mississippi River is a duck hunting experience not soon to be forgotten.

11

Waterfowling the Ol' Man:
A Day on the Mississippi

It's been a tough three years. Or to be more specific, a most difficult and frustrating three duck seasons. You see, my wife and I moved to Iowa in the summer of 1997 from Washington state, a land where waterfowlers enjoy more than 100 days of duck hunting each year. A place where bag limits are liberal and hunting pressure is often non-existent. It's a place where four – no, maybe five lifetimes wouldn't provide enough time to hunt over a spread of decoys on even 10 percent of the public wetlands.

But here in Iowa, my decoys and layout boats have, since '97, simply sat and gathered dust. Three consecutive warm winters had all but eliminated any type of migration. Too, low water levels over much of the state worked to concentrate the hoards of duck hunters and duck hunter wanna-bes on the few remaining wetland areas and, well, my Czechoslovakian background, what little there is of it, doesn't mesh well with overcrowded marshes. To fill the void, we turned to other things like turkeys, whitetails, and pheasants; however, and while our oldest black lab all but forgot what ducks were, we nonetheless missed waterfowling.

Enter Tony Toye. We first heard tell of Toye while hunting spring snow geese in southwest Iowa during March of 1998. This was the same year – in fact, the same week - that the freak storm blew into the Midwest from the North and Northwest, shutting down Interstate 80 throughout much of Nebraska and Iowa, and trapping myself, my wife, a four-year-old black lab, and a five-month-old and as yet unhouse-broken lab puppy in a place called The Tall Corn Motel for five full days. Toye, we learned later, was in Iowa from his home in Wisconsin working with members of the U.S. Fish and Wildlife Service on a project which involved evaluating and possibly legalizing the use of electronic calling devices during the late – winter and spring snow goose seasons.

"You should get in touch with Tony," said Phil Bourjaily, a fellow outdoor writer and temporary inmate at The Tall Corn. "He hunts ducks on the Mississippi, with canvasbacks being his specialty. You should look into it." At the time, however, all we wanted to look at was our own driveway.

Here we jump ahead some three and one-half years. It's late October in the New Millennium, and we're still frustrated with Iowa waterfowling. That, however, was about to change, thanks to Tony Toye and an incredible body of water known as the Mississippi River.

"Tony? M.D. Johnson. Say, my wife and I are working on a waterfowl hunting book, and we need to shoot some photography of folks hunting divers. We understand you're somewhat of a specialist when it comes to hunting canvasbacks there on the river. Any chance of hooking up with you and spending some time behind some can blocks?" And it was true. We had contracted to write and illustrate our first book, a modern yet traditional waterfowling how-to, and while we had plenty of film depicting dozens upon dozens of hunts featuring any number of different puddle duck species, our stocks were severely limited when it came to anything to do with divers.

"You come up the end of the month," said Toye, "and we'll see what we can do."

Monday, 30 October. Fortunately I'd seen, and Julie, my wife, had grown up around Washington's awesome Columbia River, because for those who haven't had the privilege of seeing such an expanse, the first look at the Mississippi is truly breath-taking. High, craggy shoreline bluffs edged in yellows, golds, and reds provided an obvious reminder to us both that we certainly weren't in inland Iowa any longer. Every dozen miles or so, tiny riverfront towns, most only a main street and a set of railroad tracks, sprouted signs that read "Dew Drop Inn," "Bill's Tavern," or "Smoked Carp Sold Here." Upstream and down, the diesel haze from passing barges, pushing cans to destina-

The canvasback decoys, 100 in all, went into the water first.

Can blocks were set out in two distinct groups, with a landing zone or hole left between the two.

Tony Toye unwraps his secret weapon, a Robo-Duck motorized decoy. For many, the jury's still out on the case regarding the effectiveness of these new spinning wing blocks.

tions only their captains knew, brought a smile of Evergreen State nostalgia to our faces. It was, as Julie said quietly, a brief glimpse at home only 100 miles away.

Earlier that morning, the four of us – Julie, myself, Toye, and his three-legged chocolate lab, Deacon – had launched Toye's sled at a very well-maintained ramp at Ferryville on the Wisconsin side of the river, and had made the brief run, out and slightly upstream, to an incredibly natural-looking, man-made island. After two attempts to conceal the big boat, the blind proved not only difficult but futile due to the high winds and waves; Toye opted for a quieter location some 200 yards to the west. Quickly, the guide and I maneuvered the boat onto the upstream point of a very small island, and while Julie positioned what Toye called "witch's brooms" – clumps of foxtail and other native grasses zip-tied around long dry posts – strategically around the boat, Toye and I began to set out the decoys. First, a "blob," as the guide called it, of smaller canvasback decoys, approximately 50 in all, were arranged running out and upstream from the stern of the boat. This spread was continued with another 30 or so magnum canvasback decoys. A hole was left between the two groups to serve as a landing area. Puddle duck decoys, primarily mallards with an old black duck or two thrown in for what I figured was the sake of tradition, were then set directly off the upstream or starboard side of the blind. Additional puddlers, along with four Canada goose floaters, were then spread randomly off the bow. As a finishing touch, Toye

posted two RotoDucks, one at either end of the blind. The rigging was completed by running the motion decoy leads – no six-volt batteries here. These electric ducks are powered by a 12-volt, deep-cycle marine battery which *does not* lack for juice! – into the boat and plugging them into their respective jacks. A couple padded boat seats, a little arranging of gear and calls, and we, as Toye said, were open for business.

Almost immediately, Julie and I knew that this wasn't going to be our typical Midwestern duck hunt. First, we were seeing ducks. Second, we were seeing lots of ducks. And third, and most surprisingly, we could only see one other boat, and they weren't within 500 yards of our position. We couldn't hear them call, and without binoculars, we couldn't even see them unless they got out of their blind to play in the decoys. After three years of hair-pulling and teeth-gnashing, we could have pulled up then and gone home, and I would have been a very, very happy guy.

But it wasn't nearly over. The first drake can, one of a two-hen, one-drake trio, fell to our host's Benelli within 10 minutes of the opening bell. Two drake mallards and a gadwall later, I had, for the first time in 26 years of waterfowling, the opportunity to tag a drake canvasback. As the bull splashed down among the decoys, it was high fives, handshakes, and a hearty hug from Julie – which, by the way gentlemen, is an incredible benefit of hunting with your significant other. By noon, we'd seen several thousand ducks, including a beautiful flock of cans that

Toye perches his spinning wing decoys on tall conduit poles, each some 6 feet or so above the water. On the Mississippi, visibility from a distance is vital to success.

Success! The author with his first drake canvasback – 26 years in the making, and all thanks to the mighty Mississippi.

caught us all flat-footed, goldeneyes, buffleheads, and even one small group of sprig, and had managed, despite some accuracy trauma, to add another pair of drake mallards and a gorgeous gray duck to our bag.

Back at the ramp, once all the film had been shot, we arranged and rearranged and re-rearranged the eight birds, and agreed between ourselves that our faith had indeed been restored in waterfowling the Midwest. Toye, a relatively quiet fellow, every now and then glanced over and smiled a knowing, "told you so" type of smile. He'd seen us before, probably a hundred times over the handful of years he'd guided on the big river. We were the resurrected, the appeased – all thanks to a talented young man, a three-legged dog, and a fascinating experience called the Mississippi River.

Mississippi divers 101

I was raised by a puddle duck man, a now-retired high school biology teacher who cut his waterfowling eyeteeth on the hoards of mallards, blacks, and wood ducks that both made their home and passed through his tiny corner of northeastern Ohio during the late 70s and early 80s. Times have changed somewhat for my father. Many of the marshes that still remain in the northern part of the Buckeye State, those untouched by tile, brick, and the developer's hand, have changed ownership to the point where the old farmers, the "Of course you can hunt

Toye and his chocolate lab, Deacon, sit back and await the arrival of the morning's flight.

here again. Now stop asking me, will ya!" kind of folks that were of my father's time and era, are now only memories and names on stones. Oh, he still finds a mallard or two along the Mahoning River, and there's more geese, he says, than he can remember; however, I digress.

It's not that my father, Mick, had anything against divers. Actually, he never gave them much thought. And, being a product of his outdoor instruction, neither did I. Truth was, we saw very few divers in the flooded pin oak swamps and cattails marshes of my native Ohio. Oh, there was the odd bufflehead or two on the Mahoning every winter, tiny little tuxedo-clad, teal-sized birds that I recognized from years of reading Ducks at a Distance.

Eager to please and entertain, this hen canvasback swam around the decoys for the better part of an hour.

Meticulously crafted, Toye's boat blind quickly becomes just another small grass island on the Mississippi. Or so it seems.

Few meals can compare to bacon and eggs in a duck blind on the Mississippi. A culinary masterpiece!

And occasionally we'd see, or more precisely hear, a passing flock of goldeneyes as we fished Lake Erie in the early fall for that last-chance big walleye of the year. But to purposely hunt divers? Hell, I didn't even own a duck call until I was in my mid-20s as, according to my father's teaching, "they're either going to be here. Or they're not."

So it was with more than 20 years of waterfowling experience, and yet probably fewer than 20 minutes of total diver duck hunting time that Julie and I made our first sojourn to the banks of the famed Mississippi River. Fortunately, Toye is accustomed to answering any of the 1,001 questions that come with what can only be described as this incredible and most traditional of waterfowling artforms, one of the most often-asked being *the* single most important element to diver hunting success on the Mississippi. His answer, even to a puddle duck man such as myself, came as little surprise.

"Location. I mean if you put out a big enough decoy spread, you can pick up a diver or two. But if you're in the best spot with a huge decoy spread, it can be a case of 'Don't touch your gun barrel 'cause it's too hot.' It's just all location," said Toye.

Location. That sounds elemental enough; however, when one considers Toye's home pool on the Mississippi, Pool 9, runs more than 25 river miles and contains literally hundreds of thousands of publicly accessible waterfowling opportunities, the word location – translation:

where – takes on an altogether different and potentially frustrating meaning. With that said, how then does Toye go about separating the good from the bad?

"The way we scout is by truck. We'll just drive looking for a good group of cans close enough to shore. There's probably six or seven good miles along this side (Ferryville, Wisconsin) of the river that you can see well from the road. And the other (Iowa) side is all refuge, so it's basically all or nothing along this side. The other thing is that you have to be in the exact spot where the birds were when you first saw them. That's the spot where the birds are going to decoy," said Toye.

Following the day on the river with Toye, it became all too apparent that while hunting divers, and particularly the famed canvasback, is a most traditional activity, it is also one wrought with misconceptions. Two of the ones that I boarded the boat carrying and which were both quickly dispelled concerned the theories that successful diver hunting is (1) a deep-water undertaking, and (2) best done over open – as in nothing around for miles and miles – water.

As Toye explained, Pool 9 is one of the shallower pools on the Mississippi River, averaging from three to six feet in depth throughout all but the main shipping channel. Years spent in scuba gear, equipment which was a necessary part of his one-time career as a commercial clammer on the river, provided Toye with an incredible amount of

Organization, both inside and outside of the boat, is vital to both the success and safety of a big river waterfowling trip.

invaluable information concerning the Mississippi's depth and bottom structure, as well as volumes of details dealing with the wide variety of natural plant and animal foods that make up the diet not only of the canvasbacks and other divers that frequent the pool, but the assortment of puddle duck species also found there throughout the year.

"The primary food for the cans here on the pool is wild celery, with fingernail clams and zebra mussels next in line," said Toye, who explained that it does surprise many of his clients the first time he jumps from the bow of the boat in the middle of such a huge expanse of river, only to have the water often barely be hip-deep.

The second statement, that being the divers and open-water theory, is both true and false on the Mississippi. Or at least on the Wisconsin portion of it. It's true, certainly, that canvasbacks and other divers are indeed fond of the wide-open spaces, and any late October or early November drive along western Wisconsin's Highway 35 will provide views of huge rafts of canvasbacks, tens of thousands of birds strong, balled up and riding the flow, all hundreds of yards from anything that could even remotely be considered cover. This natural avian tendency, coupled with Wisconsin's current open-water refuge law which requires waterfowlers on the Mississippi to hunt no more than 100 feet from the shore, an island, or any type of live, natural vegetation that provides at least partial concealment – a somewhat vague condition that can and often does differ from day to day and boat to boat – does serve a purpose, says Toye,

that being the creation of a safe haven from which the birds, divers and puddlers alike, cannot be pushed or, in the waterfowler's vernacular, burnt out.

Such species-specific characteristics and regulatory measures require hunters such as Toye to improvise and adjust, hunting the open water from boats and blinds hidden among the cattails, switchgrass, cane, and blow-downs in much they same way they would a secluded backwater or inland slough. With, of course, one major exception. This slough is 25 miles long, a mile or more wide, and can, at the right time, hold more than a quarter of a million canvasbacks within its banks.

And what crash course in big river diver hunting would be complete without some mention of decoys and decoy rigs? Enter misconception number three – A successful diver hunt includes 1.42 million decoys, each the size of a Volkswagen, and all rigged with some sort of specialized multi-block anchoring system that incorporates both bricks and cinder blocks.

"My decoy spreads consist of about 120 floaters. All magnum-sized (Editor's note: So that part is true). I use half mallards and half canvasbacks. On the side of the blind toward the open water, I'll have what I call a big 'blob' of cans. I'll leave a 15- to 20-yard gap leading downwind, and then I'll place a string of decoys. This looks like a small flock of cans that have just landed and are swimming to join the larger group. On the other side, I'll put a big bunch of feeding mallards. With the mallards, I'll use a few pintails and other species, just for color. Same with the cans.

The ultimate weapon, grassed and ready for the hanger.

I'll use a few bluebills and redheads off to the side," said Toye. As a final tactical note, not only does Toye use magnum-sized decoys in approximately one-half of his canvasback spread, he also uses *only*, as in 100 percent, drake cans in his spread. His theory, and one which he's proved year after year, is not only does size mean visibility on the big river, but the predominantly white drake cans – like drake pintails in a puddle duck spread – attract attention from far, far away. And that's important when you're dealing with something as big as the Old Man.

If you go

Tony Toye is a borderline perfectionist, which, for a Type A, anal-retentive person such as myself, is a wonderful bonus. His equipment is top-notch, and his abilities among the finest in the Midwest. While he certainly will let his people assist with the almost infinite number of duties necessary to put on such a hunt, he also knows what needs to be done *and* how he wants it done.

With Toye, safety is of the utmost concern, and ranks as Priority One, both on the water and off. Prior to the first round being chambered, the guide goes through his on-board safety requirements, which include fields of fire, gun-handling, dog reminders, and other items. During the hunt, shotgun barrels are safely locked away in no-mar rubber clips – without question an excellent idea; however, the clips do take some getting used to when it comes time to "take 'em." Fortunately, Toye went

through the process with Julie and me a couple times which, though beneficial, effectively eliminated my pre-fab "I couldn't get the gun out" excuse.

Hunts are conducted from a roomy, 18-foot I believe, plate boat powered by a smooth-running, 90-horsepower Mercury outboard. Toye has done a fantastic job of camouflaging his skiff, and waterfowlers from coast to coast will walk away with literally dozens of gear and gadget ideas, many of which the guide has designed and implemented himself.

Toye begins hunting the Mississippi in mid-October and continues through the close of Wisconsin's season in early December. Traditionally, the best time for canvasbacks is the last week in October and the first week in November, when more than 250,000 of the majestic birds will raft on this section of the Upper Mississippi River. And while cans provide the major draw for many of Toye's clients, other ducks, including mallards, blacks, widgeon, gadwall, teal, scaup, goldeneyes, redheads, and buffleheads, are all on the menu.

For pricing, scheduling, or just enough story-telling to whet any waterfowler's appetite, hunters can contact Toye by writing Big River Guide Service, 43605 CTH E, Boscobel, WI 53805, or calling 608-375-7447. He can also be reached electronically at ***toyedecoys@tds.net***.

Oh, and by the way, don't let anyone tell you that scrambled eggs and bacon taste better anywhere than they do when eaten on a duck boat in the middle of the Mississippi River. I can vouch for that one personally.

12

Productive
Public Places

*"Right here's where I was yesterday. We can stay here,
or we can move around the corner. I saw a bunch of
ducks wanting to land over there yesterday."*

Just the mere fact that friend and frequent shooting companion, Phil Bourjaily, had convinced me to travel any distance in what I considered the duckless state of Iowa was notable in and of itself. What made my participation in the event even more astounding was the fact that the morning's shoot, what there would be of it, was taking place on a notoriously crowded public wildlife area. Located between two of The Hawkeye State's larger population centers, the public lands surrounding Coralville Reservoir attracted scores of what can only be described as "interesting" – my phrase, not Bourjaily's – individuals, many of whom, based on appearance, action, and demeanor, could only vaguely be called hunters.

"My gosh, that's a lot of ducks," said Bourjaily, always quick with an understatement. It was indeed a lot of ducks. As we rounded the corner, AquaPods in tow, we startled some 300 mixed mallards, widgeon, gadwall, and teal into flight, all of which had been sitting on the lee side of a tiny point of soggy ground and grass. "That looks like the spot," said Bourjaily, who in his excitement had somehow managed to get his small paddle-powered skiff up on plane.

I guess what happened next could only be described as classic in every sense of the word. Even before we'd covered the Pods with smartweed and remnants of the year's millet planting, small knots of birds were already returning. Decoy placement became a neoprene-clad version of Twister, as I scurried and bobbed and weaved, simultaneously trying to hide and hurry and throw. Forty minutes later, Bourjaily was finished, three beautiful

drake mallards and an equally impressive trio of green-wing teal gracing the bow of his boat. Alongside my hip, two green-wings and three mallards were arranged.

"Hello?" It was my wife, Julie, at home having opted to stay and coordinate a pile of photography whilst I went and played with Bourjaily.

"You've got to come down here," I whispered into the cell phone after a brief but very descriptive telling of the morning's events. "Just turn west off the hard road at the bay where we fish and follow the gravel until you see the pickup. We'll come and get you. Dress warm and bring coffee."

An hour later, I was trading Bourjaily for my Advantage Wetlands-draped wife – a most excellent bargain on my part. For the next 60 minutes, I had the pleasure of watching my partner drop in quick succession one each mallard, gadwall, and green-wing teal, as well as one of the prettiest bull sprig this side of the Missouri River. It was, as Bourjaily agreed later, nothing short of phenomenal.

"And the best part," he added, "was that there wasn't another hunter within a mile of us. We were alone." Again, Mister Understatement was correct; however, in this case, alone was a very, very good thing.

Public hunting area. To many, just the words send a shiver of fear down the length of their spine. Conjured up are images of shoulder-to-shoulder blinds, boat ramps that look like a parking lot at the mall, and watercraft in numbers and description large enough to rival the Normandy invasion armada. It's arguments at the launch and heart-to-heart discussions in the field. Sky-painting artists who honestly believe that modern shotguns are

Dawn on a wildlife management area in eastern Iowa. Success, or chaos?

true 150-yard devices. All in all, it's a terrible thing. An ugly thing. Or is it?

Like anything else, public hunting areas have both their good points and their not-so-good points; however, here, in the section called Productive Public Areas, it's my goal to focus on the positive instead of the negative. Those aspects of waterfowling on the nation's public hunting areas that indeed make them a worthwhile proposition instead of the total waste of time and ultimate lesson in frustration that so many might believe them to be. That said, let me issue a disclaimer, for lack of a better term, and say that, no, not every public hunting experience will be a good nor a memorable one; still, there are very fine hunts to be had, all thanks – yes, indeed - to the country's public hunting areas.

Public places defined

Elemental, this defining of public hunting areas? Perhaps, but only to some extent. True, in its most basic sense, the phrase 'public hunting area' translates into a place whereon the general public may hunt. Kind of like deciphering Latin, eh? And while this definition may not be incorrect, technically speaking, it's also not complete in terms of what constitutes a perhaps slightly more accurate title for such acreages, that being 'public hunting option.'

To explain. Most waterfowlers are familiar with what many state fish and wildlife agencies call wildlife man-

agement areas. These are simply parcels of land, water or otherwise, that in some manner have come to be owned by the state. Or more precisely, by the people of that state who are then free, with restrictions of course, to use the land and the resources as they see fit. Practically without exception, these areas provide a diverse setting, often both from a wildlife, game and non-game species included, as well as a geographical or topographical standpoint. Interestingly enough, there seems to be no set minimum or maximum size for these public areas. A waterfowl production area in South Dakota, for instance, may cover only one or two acres, while Arkansas' famed Bayou Meto Wildlife Management Area, a legendary wetland as synonymous with waterfowl hunting and greenhead mallards as is anything or anyplace on the planet, encompasses more than 33,000 acres. Truth is, though, that despite the huge stature gap between the puddle in South Dakota and the puddle near Stuttgart, the size of the area does and doesn't make a difference, a point to be discussed at length later in the chapter.

Some of the more popular names for these public lands include wildlife management area, wildlife or waterfowl production area, conservation area, public hunting area, recreation areas, and heritage areas. And the list goes on and on depending upon the part of the country. Regardless, however, of what they're called, the premise is the same – land owned by the people for the people. The hunting public. And here, I believe, is a good time to make mention of the one qualifier that sets this

Because water levels on many public waterfowl grounds are controlled by area personnel, such places can provide excellent gunning even during times of drought or low water.

particular category of public lands apart from the others mentioned. This is that such management areas, at least in the past, were obtained and are currently managed, maintained, and regulated with the consumptive user, the hunter, the trapper, and the angler in mind. As you will see, that's not the case on all public lands; in fact, on some lands the consumptive user, the waterfowler included, is in a minority position so low as to damn near be non-existent.

Though numerous and found to some degree in each of the 50 states, these state-owned properties are but one option available to the waterfowler limited to or looking for opportunities on such free-to-roam parcels. Other possibilities detailed and defined include:

Restricted public hunting areas – Some public hunting areas can only be loosely defined as such as waterfowling opportunities are available only or in part on a limited pre-drawing basis. Typically, these lands are under the control and management of the state fish and wildlife agency through whom hunters must go in order to participate in the annual or season-long lottery-style drawings. Ohio's Magee Marsh, a fabulous wetland along the Lake Erie shoreline, is one such example of a drawing-type hunt, as is Iowa's Lake Odessa. These so-called public areas can indeed provide excellent waterfowling and some, like Odessa, in all fairness do offer a portion of the area on a no-drawing, walk-in basis; however, many find such lotteries to be restricting and far too competitive.

State parks and reservoirs – In many states, annual drawings are held for blinds or blind locations along lakes, rivers, streams, ponds, marshes, or other wetlands which fall within park boundaries. Often, these drawings are conducted not by the state fish and wildlife agency, but rather the department of parks or natural areas. Deadlines for such drawings are frequently in late summer, with the months of August and September being good bets. Information concerning such opportunities can usually be obtained by contacting the state Department of Natural Resources.

National Wildlife Refuges – Currently a source of controversy among many waterfowlers who contend that the unbroken chain of off-limits, no hunting refuges which presently stretches from Canada south to the traditional waterfowl wintering areas in Texas, Louisiana, and Arkansas, has negatively impacted the regulated consumptive harvest of both ducks and geese. True or not, refuges such as Wisconsin's Horicon National Wildlife Refuge (NWR), Illinois' Crab Orchard, and California's Sacramento Valley and Klamath Basin complexes without question short-stop and hold incredible numbers of migrating waterfowl, many throughout the whole of the duck and goose season. Still, many of these refuges not only allow regulated hunting, but actually cater quite well to the waterfowler. Most, like Washington's Ridgefield NWR, limit the number of hunters through the use of a lot-

Washington's Ridgefield National Wildlife Refuge, just one of many refuges across the country that allow waterfowl hunting.

Often, refuge area blinds are large and reasonably well-camouflage – the perfect setting for introducing new or young hunters to the sport.

tery-style drawing and specific blind assignments. And, too, most if not all charge some type of day-to-day or annual hunting fee; however, such refuge hunts can at times prove very productive, both from a harvest standpoint as well as from the point of "the number of things seen."

Other federal and governmental lands – National wildlife refuges are not the only federal lands that may provide an option to the enterprising waterfowler. Some of these alternatives include properties owned by –

> *Bureau of Land Management* – Maintains over 264 million acres, primarily within 12 Western states. Contact the Bureau at **www.blm.gov/**, or 202-452-5125
>
> *Bureau of Reclamation* – A section of the U.S. Department of the Interior. Visit **www.usbr.gov/** for various district information.
>
> *U.S. Army Corps of Engineers* – Water-related issues among others. Maps, invaluable tools for the waterfowler, can be obtained by visiting the Web site at **www.usace.army.mil**, clicking "Where we are," then "Looking for maps" before going into the various state and regional district public affairs offices.

> *Tennessee Valley Authority* – The Tennessee Valley Authority, or TVA, is headquartered in Knoxville, and oversees lands and waters in parts of Tennessee, Mississippi, Alabama, and Kentucky. Information is via the Internet at **www.tva.gov**, or by telephone at 865-632-2101.

Private/public – While living in Washington, I was introduced to the concept of private lands open to the public for the purposes of outdoor recreation, one of which I discovered was some fantastic and often unpressured duck hunting. Among one of the largest landholders, not only in the Pacific Northwest but in the country, with properties open to the public is the Weyerhaeuser Timber Corporation; however, others include Champion, Georgia Pacific, and many more. Most state fish and wildlife agencies can provide information regarding these private/public waterfowling opportunities.

Success, and public lands waterfowl

Successful waterfowling on public hunting areas involves a number of different elements, one of which I will openly admit is luck. Or more precisely, being in the proverbial right place at that well-known but far too elusive correct time. Over the years, I've enjoyed episodes of this "right place/right time" factor, including but not limited to a fantastic mid-morning migration day hunt for blue-wing teal in Iowa, an unforgettable outing in southwest Washington when my wife and I saw what could have only been every pintail on the planet, and an equally as enjoyable adventure on the Mahoning River in northeastern Ohio during an afternoon when shooting partner, Joe Hassman, and I couldn't have kept the mallards and blacks out of our 10-duck decoy spread with two tennis rackets and the whole of the U.S. Marine Corps Band. These events, though not devoid of planning and logistics, were more a result of the birds being there at the same time we were. Or vice versa.

Still, luck only plays a percentage of this thing called public waterfowling success. There are other variables, all much more within the grasp and control of the individual than is luck, that play an even larger, more significant role. Some, such as scouting, are part of each and every hunt. Or at least should be. Others, timing for instance, may not prove as consistently – key word: consistently - critical to the success or lack thereof of an outing. Nonetheless, each element is important in its own way. And each, or for that matter, all, can on any given day spell the difference between birds that work and no birds at all.

Many of the nation's rivers provide top-notch public waterfowling opportunities. This hunter has found success on the Mahoning River in northeastern Ohio.

Timing – When you hunt any public area is often as important as where you hunt. Weekdays, otherwise known as workdays, offer some of the finest and least competitive public hunting opportunities available. True, many folks have commitments, otherwise known as work, Monday through Friday; however, that's exactly what makes these days the best in terms of low hunter numbers. What all this means is that if at all possible, hunt through the week. If you have it and you're able, plan a portion of your annual vacation in Tuesday through Thursday, undoubtably the least active times on most wildlife areas, blocks. Can't make it through the week? Saturdays and Sundays are better than no days at all; still, it's suggested that you try to stay away from the holiday weekends such as Veteran's Day, Thanksgiving, Christmas, and the like. The time of day, too, can make a world of difference when it comes to competition at the ramp. Waterfowlers, crepuscular creatures that they are, can be found most active at sunrise and sunset. Certainly, the birds, too, will be similarly active at these times; however, there's often a period between, say, 10:00 AM and 2:00 PM when there will be a second bout of bird movement. Human movement, too, will often increase now, as those hunters who put out before dawn head back to the ramp and the warmth of their rigs and favorite restaurants. With this in mind, many public land devotees will often sleep in, not heading into the field until the hunter exodus begins and the 10 o'clock flight commences.

When possible, camping close to a public fowling opportunity can put the hunter in the best possible place in the shortest amount of time.

Scouting – It's hard, not impossible, but difficult in this day and age to find anything that even remotely resembles a "secret spot" on a modern public wetland. Local hunters, those folks who grew up practically living on the area, will very likely know each and every inch of the parcel, including where the birds are on any given day, how they leave, when they return. Chances are they'll know what's good in November and what's good in December. And they'll chuckle amongst themselves at the new folks as they watch them arrange a beautiful spread on what they refer to as the "No Duck Hole." And to a large extent, that's what it takes in order to be successful on today's public waterfowing areas. In-depth scouting. Whether it's done over a period of years, weeks, or days, it really doesn't matter. What does matter is (a) that it's done, and (b) that it's done as completely and as thoroughly as possible. But what if you're like most folks who put in an honest 40-plus hours of hard work each week? How then do you get such in-depth scouting done? Truth is, there's nothing that will nor can replace actual time spent in the field – walking, watching, drawing, noting – but there are indeed several ways to maximize the efficiency of the time that you do have to devote to this all-important variable.

Timing, otherwise known as a hunt during the week, was the key to this lone hunter's success on this small public pond in western Iowa.

1. **Use and believe in maps.** Maps are probably the single most oft-forgotten resource or reference tool available to the waterfowler looking to spend time on public wetlands. And why? Many hunters, myself included, fall into what can only be called a rut in terms of location. Year after year, season after season, we hunt the same areas – some not only the same general area, but many the same quarter-acre patch of ground – because, understandably, these areas have produced in the past. But what about those years when they don't produce? Maybe there's another part of the same complex that the birds *are* using. Or perhaps there's another similar public area just five short miles away that would be much more productive. Maps – surprise! – can provide this information, or at least the alternative location information, even before the season begins. Most state fish and wildlife agencies can supply detailed maps of their holdings, as can many federal outfits such as the U.S. Fish and Wildlife Service, the Corps of Engineers, and the Bureau of Land Management. Map-makers such as the DeLorme Mapping Company of Freeport, Maine, who produce an incredible series of conveniently designed state-by-state topographic maps in their Gazetteers and Atlases, can also serve as a jumping-off point for hunters looking to do their geographic homework. Taking this one step further, DeLorme also makes available a complete state-specific set of topographic maps on compact disk (CD) for those scouters who would rather start their search in front of their PC.

2. **Ask questions.** It's surprising the number of hunters who year after year spend much of their time on a piece of public ground, and have never once talked with the area manager or their local waterfowl biologist, both sources of some of the most up-to-the-minute, accurate, area-specific hunting information available. Over the years, it's been my experience that refuge managers and regional biologists are a friendly, happy-to-help lot. Most are far removed, or at least far enough removed, from the politics and the bureaucracy of the central office or the state seat of wildlife government, with most then feeling free and comfortable to talk openly and honestly about the area, its good points, and its not-so-good points. Time spent in conversation with such individuals – before, after, and during the season - is definitely time well-spent, and can provide details and information concerning such things as future wetland projects, regulatory changes, closures, openings, and yearly agricultural plans – all items which can very easily prove most informative when hunting season once again rolls

Many public areas require hunters to walk into their blind locations, a physical fact that – fortunately - leaves many standing at the gate.

Here, the author and Maggie found uncrowded conditions on this western Washington public area, thanks to the easy and far-from-the-parking-lot access provided by their AquaPod.

around. Another possible benefit to such a conversation is information dealing with prospective private-lands waterfowling opportunities on properties in close proximity to the manager's or supervisor's own state or federally-owned territory. Remember, it never, ever hurts to ask.

3. **The Internet.** For those with access – and who doesn't have access these days? – the Internet can be a phenomenal source of scouting information. Through Web sites such as ***www.waterfowler.com***, All Outdoors' (***www.alloutdoors.com***) waterfowler's forum, and a long and ever-growing list of local, state, regional, and national sites, duck hunters are able to track with reasonable though differing accuracy, important variables such as fall migrations, hunting pressure, state agency updates, and weather patterns. Public areas, too, are a common topic of conversation on such sites and their accompanying chat rooms. And those 'Net surfers capable of looking, listening, and separating the truth from the BS, an art that isn't always easy to accomplish, can find themselves armed with some very valuable public lands information. The 'Net can also be used to access most, if not all, of the state fish and wildlife agencies, as well as federal and other governmental

offices. At such departmental sites, browsers will find state-by-state listings of waterfowl biologists or project leaders, current aerial surveys and counts, state or regional field reports; in fact, an astonishing conglomeration of information the likes of which duck hunters have never before been offered. All you have to do is go online, and take advantage of the technology.

Hunt hard – Sure, comfort's nice. A heated blind, a dry seat, a mud-free environment. However, comfort does not always coincide with a hefty duck strap. In fact and in my experience, it's quite the opposite. An inverse relationship, so to speak, that translates into a sort of proportion involving misery and success. But what does this mean to the fowler looking to hunt a piece of public ground *and* get away from the competition? Simple. Hunt hard. The more willing you are to walk the extra mile, use the off-beat boat ramp, get muddy, work harder, and stay miserable, chances are the more successful you will be from a harvest standpoint. Case in point. Low water levels at eastern Iowa's Hawkeye Wildlife Area, a huge impoundment on the Iowa River, had all of the state's boat-bound duckers and most of the stick-blind hunters up in arms. The vegetation, it seemed, was far too short to hide their boat blinds, canoes, jon boats, and the armada of stay-dry, stay-clean skiffs and hides that annually dotted the reser-

Need to get away from the crowd? Why not try a small boat or canoe?

While perhaps not the best weather-wise for the duck hunter, bluebird days can help cut the competition down dramatically, as photographer Julie Johnson shows.

voir during Iowa's brief September duck season. Hoards of migrating blue-wing teal, on the other hand, were enjoying themselves to no end on the shallow, bug-filled waters. Were they out of reach? Not to me and a pair of friends who made the quarter-mile walk/wade from the ramp to the millet-covered flats and sat on our neoprene-covered butts in the mud, surrounded by two dozen mallard decoys. Did we get wet? Did we get muddy? Were we uncomfortable? The answer to all of the above is yes. Did we kill limits of fine-eating blue-wing teal, with the occasional green-wing, mallard, and gray duck thrown in? Yes we did.

Do something different – With the possible exception of migrating birds new to a particular area, who themselves still have seen public spread after public spread after public spread all along the flyway, the ducks that frequent public wetlands can often be best and perhaps most accurately described as jaded. In short, they know the program. They know exactly where the refuge boundaries are. And they recognize and avoid each and every blind, especially the ones surrounded with the 30-some-odd frozen, unmoving, and very unattractive fowl. What then? In such hard-to-please situations, it's often best just to do something as simple as something different. For instance, if everyone else is using a Robo-Duck, try an old-fashioned jerk cord. Simple to make and easy to use, jerk cords allow the

hunter to put those often all-important splashes and waves onto the water, something that no Robo-Duck can do. Varying the size of the decoy spread can also be productive. If possible, try 100 blocks; if not, try only four or five, one of which is a jerk cord or motion decoy of some sort. Not only can smaller spreads be tremendously effective, especially later in the year as educated birds become familiar and similarly cautious of multi-duck spreads, but I for one would much rather carry and place six decoys as opposed to 60. Or 600. Another tactic, too, is to use an "off" decoy species. In those areas with an abundance of coots, I've found two or three dozen coot decoys – yes, I said two or three dozen – to be effective. With this most interesting spread, I'll place three or four magnum mallard decoys, drakes for higher visibility, on the fringes of this conglomeration of coots. For a reason I'm sure known only to them, ducks often exhibit the frustrating habit of totally ignoring the finest decoy spreads, even bypassing live members of their own tribes, in order to land alongside a flotilla of coots. Okay, so it may appear a little goofy, this setting out of multitudinous coot decoys; however, (1) people will in all likelihood give you more than enough empty space to work with, and (2) you can always buy a dozen "name your species" decoys for $10 at a garage sale, paint them black, give them a little white bill, and presto – a coot spread.

A lone hunter walks a public marsh in eastern Iowa. In this case, lonely is just fine.

The 10 Commandments for hunting public areas

Everyone has his or her own set of commandments. Moses. Charlton Heston, who played Moses. Phil Robertson, not to be confused with Charlton Heston or Moses. The National Wild Turkey Federation. And on and on and on. And while Moses' and Phil's commandments will most certainly differ, they do share one major parcel of common ground. If, the commandments state, you follow these commandments to the letter, you will be a better person. A more successful person. A healthier person. A more complete person. Or, as is the case with this particular set of commandments, a better and more successful public lands waterfowler.

Oh, and like the original commandments, those carried by Moses and copied by Charlton, these rules are in no particular order. Number One is no more important than is Number Five. Nor can you bend Number Eight just because it's Number Eight, and therefore – theoretically – less vital in the overall scheme of things. Each is important in its own right.

1. **Thou shalt not shoot another man's swing.** It's very bad etiquette to shoot into a flock of ducks that are working another hunter's spread, even if the birds are, for your blind, in more-than-acceptable range. This act is known as shooting the swing, and

has resulted in countless millions of heated field debates across the country over the years.

2. **Thou shalt provide ample space between thineself and others.** This one's simple. Don't crowd your neighbor. Certainly, space can be both limited and a difficult variable to achieve on some public hunting areas; however, no one wants to have company a mere 80 yards away. The rule here is – if you think you're too close, you probably are. And if in doubt, ask the other party. Sometimes two individuals or two small groups can combine forces, thus increasing their effectiveness and decreasing the friction.

3. **Thou shalt know the effective range of thine own fowling piece.** – Odd, it's true, but there are those who believe that a 12-gauge shotgun is indeed capable of consistent 100-yard kills or that harvesting a mallard or widgeon is simply a matter of mathematics. You shoot often enough, regardless of the range, and you're bound to hit something. These are the skybusters, hunters in the loosest sense of the word who rate among the public hunting crowd right up there with those who would bludgeon their Grandma with a hickory stick. Fortunately, the remedy for skybusting on an individual level is easy. Know, realistically, what your firearm is capable of. Then limit yourself.

4. **Thou shalt not use a duck call non-stop, nor blow at everything in sight.** On a private marsh, it may be more than acceptable to toot on that new, "Cost me $19.95 and, damn it, I'm going to use it" duck call non-stop from sun-up to sundown. There, you're annoying no one but the dog – and if he's smart, he'll bite you. On a public wetland, however, it's best to have some consideration for your fellow hunters, their overall outdoor experience, and their ears. Sure, it's your call, it's a public area, and, damn it, you're going to use it if'n you want to. Consider the fact, though, that that same call looks a lot better hanging around your camo-clad neck than it might, well, elsewhere.

5. **Thou shalt setup and tear down quickly and effectively.** Few things aggravate a public lander more than seeing his competition show up 10 minutes before legal shooting time and having them begin the setup process some 200 yards away. The only thing that might compare is the boater who leaves the ramp at the same time, and then insists on motoring around the marsh, in and out and around decoy spreads and blinds, mere minutes – nay, seconds – before the opening bell sounds. If possible, try to arrive at your public location well in advance of legal shooting time. Once there, get yourself situated as quickly, efficiently, and effectively as possible, particularly if the situation forces you to locate within a short, say 100-200 yards, distance of another party. NOTE – For any number of reasons – work, children, home commitments, whatever – a predawn arrival may not be possible. Does this mean you don't hunt that public wetland? Certainly not; however, remember that there are folks who've been there since well before light. If you can, distance yourself both in location and travel from these early-risers. If you can't, apologize, and then get in and get setup quickly.

6. **Thou shalt not clean thine kill at the ramp. Nor at the parking lot.** Sure, every hunter has an ego to some extent. We want to show our colleagues and our competition just how effective and successful we are. There's nothing wrong with that, if it's done in moderation and with humility. However, one way not to show your hunting prowess is to clean your bag at the ramp or on the fringes of the parking lot. In fact, at any visible location. Remember, public areas are just that – public – and are used in many cases to a much greater extent by non-hunters than hunters. No one wants to see piles of feathers, innards, wings, and heads lying in the ditch. That's not macho; it's a mess.

7. **Thou shalt be familiar with and abide by the waterfowling regulations.** This goes beyond state and federal regulations to include public area-specific restrictions as well. Ignorance, despite its sporadic popularity, is no defense, nor is it any excuse for trespassing onto adjoining private property, overbagging, stretching the time limit either early or late, or any one of a thousand different "Well, I didn't know" types of situations. The bottom line is that it's your responsibility as a representative of the consumptive community *and* as a steward of our planet's natural resources to know.

8. **Thou shalt know the area boundaries and, though you may be tempted by fowl or beast, stay within them.** Let's face it. If you came home from work and there was a stranger sitting in your brown reclining chair man-handling your television remote control and helping himself to your jalapeno cheese dip, you would in all likelihood be just a little tense. In fact, there just might be an issue or two. Private land and landowners are no different. So what if there's 240 acres of it? It's still his brown reclining chair. It's all pretty elemental. Respect private property, ask permission, and respect off-limits areas such as refuge boundaries, no-shoot zones, agriculture in progress, and other common sense situations.

9. **Thou shalt leave thine temper at home.** Nobody likes a grouch, a fact which may explain why I have few friends. Same holds true for public marshes and the folks who use them. If the birds are down and the ramp's open, you can safely bet that there will be others using the same piece of public ground. Your choices, then, are two. One is to understand the competition and deal with it. "Adapt, improvise, overcome." as Clint Eastwood wisely suggested in the movie, "Heartbreak Ridge." The second option? Stay at home.

10. **Thou shalt work harder than most.** Although this particular commandment was addressed in detail earlier in the chapter, it's worth both mentioning again and including here. The secret to success on public lands is simply to work harder. If, and only if, you walk a little farther, call a little better, hide more completely, spread a few more decoys, and use your brain *as well as* your back, you'll enjoy much more good fortune on these most interesting of waterfowling arenas.

13
From Field to Feast

My father recalls, and none too fondly, the first time he brought home a limit of mallards and black ducks. Oh, the shooting and the birds themselves were fabulous. Most memorable; however, it's what happened afterwards that, well, tarnished the entire affair.

At that time – the early 70s, I believe - a relative newcomer to the art of waterfowling, my father worked laboriously hand-plucking each of the four birds he'd killed on the river that morning. "I wanted them to look nice because your Mom was going to roast them," he told me on one of the very few occasions where he felt brave enough to recount the tale. The task complete, he turned the fowl over to my mother, a good cook in her own right, to do with as she saw fit.

About halfway through the standard one hour at 350 degrees that my mother deemed sufficient, the house, my father remembers, began to fill with a odor not unlike that of a beached carp. In June. In Phoenix. Emanating from the kitchen – more precisely they discovered, the oven – the stench, as he described it, rolled through their small home like a fog. And not on little cat feet like in the Robert Frost poem, but more like the treads of a D-9 Cat. Eyes watering, and with gag reflex flexing, my father grabbed the tin foil lined cake pan and set it outside. There the foul smell hung like a bad aura. "It got on you," remembered my father.

Years later, and once my father had learned much, much more about the ways of both waterfowl and waterfowlers, he enlightened me as to the cause of the unfortunate situation. Seems the hunt took place during Ohio's, at that time, second split, a late-season opportunity that was offered each year between Christmas and New Year's. As most, if not all, of the still waters in the northeastern corner of The Buckeye State were frozen at that time, the only option open to enterprising duck

Considered by many to be the finest eating duck available, mallards do indeed rank at the top of the culinary list. But where?

hunters, not to mention any ducks that hadn't left for southern climes, were the rivers. That brief, in and of itself, lends little in way of explanation. What does help explain this most educational experience was the fact that the hoards of mallards and black ducks my father found on the Mahoning River that morning had been gorging themselves on winter-killed gizzard shad, a culinary fact my father discovered during the cleaning process and yet, still in his waterfowling infancy, failed to

Small in size, the diminutive green-wing teal certainly makes up in taste for what it might lack in stature.

connect with any possible traumatic situation. Upon the addition of heat to said waterfowl, the result, as my folks discovered, was something akin to putting a propane torch to a Twinkee filled with anchovy paste.

"It wasn't good," said my father, always the King of the understatement. "I learned a lot that day," he continued, hand poised on his 55-cent mug of draft (Remember, this was the early 70s). "I guess your mother did too."

Ducks, and the determining factors

Here's the bottom line, folks. Wild ducks are not chicken. They're not turkey nor squab nor Rock Cornish game hens. They're not pale-breasted, stay-at-homes like pheasants, quail, or grouse. What they are is hard-flying, dark-meated, unique tasting wild fowl with a flavor, an aroma, and a texture all their own. What I've told people over the past two decades about the taste of wild ducks, and geese for that matter, is this – You're either going to love it, or you're going to hate it. There seems to be no middle ground. Why, I'm not sure, but if someone says that the wild duck they're eating is "just okay," chances are they're just being polite. That, or their taste buds really are deceased. And as for what wild ducks taste like, something that folks constantly ask us to describe in detail – well, all I can tell them is that it's a little like liver, and a lot like duck.

Waterfowl, like most wild game, arrives at the dinner

table tasting as it does for a variety of reasons. With ducks, these reasons are four. They include (1) the species harvested and being prepared, (2) the manner in which these birds are – or are not – cared for in the field, (3) how the birds are handled at home, including storage practices, and (4) the way the ducks are prepared for the table. When all four variables are in synch, the Moon's aligned with Mars, and all is right with the World, wild waterfowl provide some of the finest eating available on the planet; however, if any one of the four elements is neglected or rates less than satisfactory, the end result might quite possibly be something the likes of which memories are made of – like having your appendix removed.

Species matters

How a certain duck rates on the table is a qualifier that essentially begins as soon as the bird breaks through its shell. More specifically, just what kind of duck is it? Like the differences between various wines or apples, berries or fine cigars, different species of ducks will taste differently. Just because a duck is a duck doesn't mean that it's going to eat like every other duck. Would you expect a bottle of Chateau Petrus '89 to taste just like a fifth of Mad Dog "The Wine of the Century" 20/20, simply because they're both drinks made from crushed grapes? Certainly not.

But there's more to it than that, and here's where my father's tale of culinary woe comes in. Edibility, when it comes to waterfowl depends not only on the species harvested, but what that particular bird had been eating at the time it unwisely hovered over the decoys. It's true that most puddle ducks – mallards, teal, and widgeon, for instance – consume primarily grains and grasses, with only a small percentage of their diet being made up of animal matter. Insects and spiders, and the like. This fondness for good, wholesome meals gives puddle ducks a pleasant flavor and aroma, and ranks them high in terms of taste. Conversely, it's also true that diving ducks such as scaup, ringnecks, and goldeneyes eat mostly small fish, mussels, clams, and other "living" things. This diet, unfortunately, imparts a rather poor taste to the flesh of these particular species. Like many things, however, these are but taster's guidelines when it comes to deciding between puddlers and divers – guidelines which can and do change from time to time. Remember the mallards and black ducks my father shot on the Mahoning River? These puddlers, traditionally both some of the finest-eating ducks available, had been taking advantage of the river's annual shad bonanza, an opportunity which they probably saw as being a meal or meals worthy of royalty. This choice, however, made them much less than desirable when it came time to break out the knives and forks. Similarly, some divers such as canvasbacks and redheads

The good and the not-so-good. A fine-eating puddle duck, the widgeon (top) far outshines the handsome but definitely lacking in taste hooded merganser (bottom).

It doesn't matter what variety – green-wing, blue-wing, or cinnamon – a teal by any other name tastes just as fine.

spend much of their time feeding on aquatic plants and grasses, thus making them standouts, taste-wise, among the rest of the diver family.

What, then, is the bottom line when it comes to species and taste? As a rule of thumb, puddle ducks, with few exceptions – shovelers, also known as mud ducks, being the one that comes first to mind – are usually reliable in terms of taste. Good taste, that is. Divers, on the other hand, often leave much to be desired. Still, taste is in the eye, or rather on the palate, of either the beholder or taster, with some folks who would much rather sit down to a meal of crock pot bluebills or bufflehead than they would a roasted wood duck or mallard. It's hard to conceive personally, but they're out there. And more power to them.

The species: where do they rate?

Mind you, folks, this next section is the offspring of a combination of experience and personal opinion. Nothing more. Some hunters are going to flip-flop one bird for another, while others will simply look at the following list, shake their head, and say that there's absolutely nothing that can be done to make these birds edible. Ask Phil "The Duck Commander" Robertson about the subject, and he'll tell you that all it takes is a little more garlic to make those bottom tier birds taste a whole lot better. That said, the list includes –

Puddle ducks

1. **Wood ducks** – Little ducks, whose diet of acorns, plants, seeds, and other vegetables put them at the Number 1 position on the eating list. They're sweet, and absolutely fantastic slow-roasted.

2. **Teal** – It doesn't matter if it's blue-wing or green-wing. Sure, it takes several because they're small, but what they lack in size, they surely make up for in taste. Excellent roasted or split and broiled.

3. **Mallards and blacks** – As long as they're not eating shad, one of the finest ducks available. Stuffed with orange, apple, and onion slices, they're superb.

4. **Widgeon** – The baldpate doesn't get the credit he deserves. He decoys well, likes to hear calls, and usually proves a fine-eating little duck.

5. **Gadwall** – Another bird that gets a bum rap, often just because his head isn't green and he doesn't have a little curl on his butt. Like the widgeon, the gray duck decoys and responds to a call well. Split him in half and roast him on the grill, basting often with a mix of white wine and garlic.

6. **Pintail** – He's skinny, but good nonetheless.

7. **Ringnecks** – One year in Washington, we shot a bunch of ringnecks throughout the season off a little wooded pond near the house. Broiled with a little garlic, we liked them. Some folks don't.

8. **Shovelers** – Before my wife's youngest son learned to tell the difference between the species, Robbie got all the spoonies we shot, which weren't many.

Divers, like the bluebills bagged by these hunters in eastern Washington, can be good; however, it's all in the cleaning – get rid of all the fat! – and the cooking.

A duck strap helps keep birds apart and allows rapid cooling.

Personally, I think they taste like mud. Garlic just makes them taste like mud and garlic.

Divers

1. **Canvasbacks** – It's the fact that the can tastes so incredibly good, his diet being mainly water plants and grasses, that got him into trouble with the market hunters in the early part of the 20th century. Today, he's just as good. Thank goodness he's a big duck because one's all you can have.

2. **Redheads** – Most consider redheads to be nearly as good as canvasbacks. Trick here is to slow-roast them.

3. **Bluebills** – I've eaten scaup many times by thin-slicing breast fillets and using the strips in stir-fry. A little stronger than cans, redheads, or the puddlers, but overall pretty good.

4. **The other divers** – My experience with divers like goldeneye and bufflehead is relatively limited. Some folks really like the taste of the tiny buffleheads, birds also known as butterballs. Me? I'd rather have widgeon or teal.

Field care

Over the course of the past 50 years or so, deer hunters, a notoriously hard-headed tribe, have finally come to learn and accept the fact that what comes from the kitchen in terms of the taste of any venison dish begins immediately after the animal hits the ground in the field. In some cases, actually before the animal falls. Adrenalin, lactic acid, and any number of mysterious mammalian chemicals can and will impart what many believe are less than pleasant tastes and smells to wild meat; thus, the challenge, at least in the case of a white-tail destined for the dinner table, is not only in the harvest, but in a short stalk and a clean, solitary, minimal steak-destroying shot, both followed immediately by prompt and thorough field dressing and transportation from the field. Actually, it's all rather easy – get it down, get it clean, get it cool, get it home. That's really all there is to the process. The end result? Excellent venison

What many hunters don't realize, unfortunately, is that this "don't run 'em five miles and drive 'em to town on the hood" method of caring for venison should carry over to the letter in all types of hunting situations, regardless of the game being pursued. This, to the surprise of some, includes waterfowl. There are, of course, some differences between caring for big game such as whitetails, and tending to a half a limit of mallards. Field dressing, for instance, often a weight-reducing necessity in the case of deer or other big game which must be physically – translation: dragging by hand – removed from the field to a vehicle or residence, would be considered by many hunters as a given; however, and due in large part to the fact that seldom do three mallards require two grown men and an all-terrain vehicle to get back to camp, waterfowl and field dressing aren't nearly the synonymous terms as are deer and dressing.

This said, does this mean that there are no field care suggestions or procedures for the successful waterfowler? Not true. In fact, prompt care of ducks and geese in the field can greatly add to their rating on the table. What's more, these rules as we'll call them, are relatively few in number and very black-and-white in their explanation and understanding.

Dry plucking is best accomplished by working against the grain; that is, from tail to head. Denuding the bird is an art, and does take practice. Oh, and a hefty set of thumb muscles.

1. **Match your ammunition** to both your quarry and your situation. Just like a 160-pound whitetail will be turned inside-out with a hit from a .416 Rigby, not to mention almost immediately transformed into a very interesting rendition of field deer burger, so too will a mallard bagged at 25 yards over decoys with 1⅛ ounces of BBB steel. Using the proper ammunition at the proper ranges will both result in clean, ethical harvests *and* a minimal loss of table fare.

2. **Warm weather or cold,** don't pile birds up. Especially in warm weather conditions, piling birds over the course of a morning's hunt is just asking for trouble. Consider, for a minute, a fully-feathered yet deceased mallard, a bird cleanly killed but not shot up; however, three pellets had punctured the drake's intestines. Now, put said mallard in a 100-degree oven for three hours. This, folks, is the bird or birds at the bottom of the pile. Cold weather slows the process; still, even under colder conditions, the birds at the bottom get a little warmer than need be. A better idea is to separate the birds in the field so each might cool more quickly. This can be done by simply laying the birds out individually, or by using a duck strap or tote and hanging the birds in the blind.

3. **To field dress, or not to field dress.** Very seldom over the years have I field dressed waterfowl, the only exception being hunts during which the weather was extremely warm such as an early September goose hunt. In such cases I'll simply pluck the bird around the vent area just enough to make a small incision and remove the innards before hanging the bird in the blind. Occasionally, yes, I'll pluck a bird completely in the field, most often due to the fact that the bird in my hands has been the only one I've seen all morning. If you opt for this

time-killing field cleaning method, please remember two things: (1) leave the fully-feathered head attached as required by law, and (2) don't pluck and gut birds at the boat ramp, parking area, or other public access point. Non-hunters – hell, for the matter, I – use these same areas, and a pile of duck viscera, feathers, and discarded bloody paper towels looks tacky and in no way points a finger at prowess, but rather idiocy.

4. **For transportation purposes** between the field and home or lodging, the above trio hold true. Especially the part about keeping the birds cool and protected from the elements, the dog, flies, and other potentially harmful things. Leave the fully-feathered head attached, and, if necessary, put the birds in an iced cooler for the trip.

Home – now what?

Home is where some waterfowlers, novice and veteran alike, begin to get a little tight around the edges, stymied perhaps, as to how to care for the birds at this point. Actually, preparing waterfowl either for storage or the table isn't difficult; time-consuming, maybe, but certainly not difficult.

During my formative years, my father – remember the King of the Understatement? – had a steadfast rule

In warm wather, field dressing your bird can greatly improve the end result by helping to cool your harvest quickly. Cold weather? It's your choice. Cut along the line and remove the entrails.

when it came to cleaning ducks and geese. "Pluck 'em around the butt," the Master's Degree carrying and Phi Beta Kappa key-owning guy would eloquently say, " gut 'em, and hang 'em from the end of the boat in the garage. Oh, and make sure you put more newspaper down this time. Last time we (notice the 'we' used here?) got blood on the floor, and your mother wasn't too happy with us." The process never changed, even down to the "put more newspaper down" part.

Despite the routine, my father did actually have a good method behind his madness. When the weather permitted, this being temperatures between nothing and about 40 degrees, we would take our birds, pluck them just enough to remove the innards, and hang them inside the non-heated garage for a day or two to age. And while I'm certainly not going to devote time nor space to a debate dealing with the pros and/or cons of hanging and aging wild game, let it suffice to say that the process did seem to upgrade the taste of our waterfowl, not to mention the fact that the hanging and chilling process did aid in the art of feather removal.

Which brings me to just that very point – feather removal. When it comes to separating duck from duck feathers, all waterfowlers, myself included, have both their favorite and least favorite methods. There are, I'm sure, more techniques than I'm about to discuss; however, what follows are what I'll refer to as the most popular.

1. **Dry plucking** – Every Winter about December, as I was growing up, I would notice that the muscle on the top of my hand between my thumb and forefinger had grown in size and hardness so as to resemble a flesh-colored black walnut. Or at least half of one. This was due to my participation in what was *the* only acceptable method of duck cleaning at 648 Saint Clair Avenue, that being the dry plucking method. Starting with the bird, be it duck or goose, held by the feet in the left hand, we used our on or master hand to pluck, clumps is the best way I can describe it, feathers and down from the bird's body. It seems to work most effectively going from tail to beak, or against the grain. Also, I learned through repetition that by pressing down against the bird's skin with my thumb while simultaneously pushing forward, I could pinch off both primary feathers as well as the down in one very clean fell swoop. Once the bird is denuded, a quick going-over with a propane torch removes any missed down and all those hair-like feathers that don't make for really good eating. A note here. Propane is indeed the way to go for singeing. Newspaper torches are not only less convenient, but (a) are harder to control, (b) can impart an odd taste to the bird due to the burning ink resins, and (c) have been responsible for more than one burned hand, glove, set of bangs, hat, or in the worst case scenario, an outbuilding. Fans of dry plucking might also be interested to know that commercial or mechanical pluckers, small circular devices complete with dozens of little rubber "fingers" that rotate and pull the feathers from the bird, are also available. These range from baseball-sized units that can be operated with an ordinary ⅜-inch drill as a power source to huge industrial grade machines that come with feather vacuums and 55-gallon waste disposal drums.

2. **Scalding** – We always scalded our pheasants. Unlike a duck's tough skin, a rooster's skin is very easily torn. Scalding, however, loosened the rooster's feathers somewhat, making it much easier, though much less attractive, to pluck the bird without the end result being a ragged, roadkill-esque thing. Ducks can also be scalded. Hot tap water will work; however, water that's been heated to damn near boiling seems to work even better. Simply dunk the bird two or three times, or until it's thoroughly soaked through, into the hot water being careful not to cook it. Most of the feathers, including many if not all of the wing quills, can be easily removed. Some folks say that adding a little bit of liquid dish soap to the water makes pulling the feathers from the bird easier. And while that twist

might be true, I'm not much on recipes calling for birds-and-bubbles. The downside with the scalding method is the mess and the additional step in the process; however, some hunters wouldn't have it any other way.

3. **Waxing** – Here I have to confess and say that I've never in my 26 years of waterfowling dipped a bird in hot, melted wax. Still, there are those who, like proponents of scalding, wouldn't use any other method. With the waxing method, birds are simply dipped into a special hot wax and the wax allowed to cool. Once hard, the wax, along with the feathers, can be peeled from the carcass in chunks, leaving only the finer, smaller feathers behind. The wax can then be remelted and the feathers strained in preparation for the next outing. Personally, I can't imagine the mess or the additional time involved with this technique, and I believe it's one that will eventually go the way of the point system.

4. **Skinning** – Skinning is another option open to the successful waterfowler. Unfortunately, and while skinning is without question one of the quickest methods for cleaning ducks, it's also eliminates one of the most important players in keeping the bird moist during the cooking process – the skin. To skin a duck, simply take a sharp knife and make a shallow incision from the base of the neck above the breast bone or keel, and down the sternum to the point where the thin stomach wall begins. This is between the vent and the base of the breastbone. Then, merely peel the skin in opposite directions away from the centerline. Continue to slide the skin away from the body, separating it with your fingers where necessary, to the point where you've almost encircled the bird. Next, disjoint and cut away the wings at the body. This requires some practice and a little bending, but gets easier with time. Now, taking your knife, cut through the stomach wall and backbone, but leave the tail attached to the skin. Grab the tail and pull it toward the head, collecting both wings and wingbones in the process. Peel the skin, tail, wings, and all up to the neck, and cut free.

5. **Filleting** – Filleting begins much the same way as does skinning, with a shallow incision from the neck, down the breast bone, to the end of the keel above the stomach wall. The next step is to expose both breast halves, just as you did in the skinning process, by sliding and working the skin off the breasts and around to the sides. Now, with the bird lying on its back, insert the point of a sharp fillet knife on one side, left or right, of the 'V' at the bot-

Filleting both ducks and geese (breasts only) is a quick and efficient cleaning method, particularly if large numbers of birds are involved.

tom of the bird's wishbone. Push the blade down until you contact bone, and then slide the knife along the keel to the bottom. Repeat on the opposite side. Next, turn the blade *toward* the bird's beak and, starting at the original cut, work the blade along both the left and right sides of the wishbone. Done correctly, the cut will look just like the letter 'Y.' To finish, grab the corner of the fillet at the point of the wishbone and pull the meat away from the centerline. A little bit of knife work will separate the boneless fillet from both the ribs and the breast plate. Again, repeat on the other side. A cut prepared as such is now ready to be marinated in Italian dressing, wrapped in bacon, and grilled. Or thin-sliced for stir fry. Or maybe thicker sliced for jerky. The bottom line is, it's all good eating.

If you're planning on eating your birds straight away, then the subject of storage is of no concern; however, if duck isn't immediately on the menu, then the question of how to keep your harvest nice and fresh for an indefinite period of time comes to the forefront.

After years of Ziploc bags and milk containers filled with frozen water-and-duck, neither of which worked really well, my wife and I finally bought one of the commercial vacuum sealers. The result? An almost total lack of freezer burn and no noticeable decrease in taste or texture, even after a year or more in the freezer. These food-

A hunter preparing Blind Duck, small chunks of seasoned breast fillet skewered on willow sticks and quick-broiled over a charcoal hobo oven. An excellent mid-morning break.

suckers work well for sealing either whole birds or fillets, as well as packaging smoked birds or slices of smoked waterfowl for use as decorative and out-of-the-ordinary Christmas presents or any-time-of-year gifts. And while, yes, they're a bit on the expensive side, one of these units will more than pay for itself within a season or two given the price of Ziplocs and all the other gizmos and gadgets out there which claim to keep game and fish as fresh as the day it was killed or caught. The only way to do that? Eat it that day, or lead it home on a leash and tie it out in the yard until dinner.

The end of chaos in the kitchen

Waterfowl recipes can be as simple or as complex as one's taste buds dictate; however, two rules of thumb hold true regardless of how the birds are prepared for the table – (1) moist, and (2) rare. Or at the very most, medium rare. Better yet, on the rare side of medium rare. Either way, this pair of factors, remembered, will result in excellent waterfowl time and time again. Forgotten? How about the words "shoe leather."

Every duck hunter has his or her favorite recipe. And there's nothing wrong with that; however, and I too am guilty of this, there should be some consideration given to trying something new, not necessarily exotic but new, from time to time. Experimentation over the years

has led me and my waterfowling cohorts to some of the world's finest recipes, along with some of the planet's worst. Among some of the former of these would be –

Grilled duck

As simple as it sounds. Take one bird per person, two birds if they're something like teal or wood ducks, and split them – the birds, not the diners – in half lengthwise. A little salt, pepper, and garlic powder on each side, and they're ready for the grill. Cook the birds, breast-side-up, on a medium-high heat almost until the juice runs clear, basting occasionally with a mixture of white wine and Italian dressing to which a few splashes of Watkins' garlic oil has been added. Flip the birds breast side down just long enough to put sear marks on them (about a minute), and serve very warm.

Barbecued duck/goose breast

In most cases, I like to barbecue my duck or goose breasts not as fillets but on the bone. This helps retain as much of the natural juices as possible; still, I'll grill whatever's taken out of the freezer.

With waterfowl breasts, be it fillets or on-the-bone, I begin with a marinade mixture of orange juice, salt, pepper, cayenne pepper, and garlic oil. The breasts are soaked for two to three hours, sometimes overnight if I'm feeling lazy. Just prior to cooking, I'll take the fillets from the brine and lightly dry. Again working with a medium-high grill, cook the fillets breast-up (bone-down) until the juice runs pink. Flip, sear, and serve with white Irish potatoes sauteed in butter with morels – or chantrells for you western folks – and garlic.

Bagley's breasts

Come on now. That's not what I'm talking about at all.

This recipe came to us from John Bagley, a good friend of ours from Austin, Texas. In the spring of 2000, Julie and I guided John and his lovely wife, Michal, on an incredible Rio Grande turkey hunt near the Pedernales River in Blanco County. Despite every effort on my behalf to scare all of Bagley's gobblers away, he managed to tag a beautiful longbearded tom. And from that bird, said John, this recipe sprang forth. Originally, John used wild turkey; however, he's since incorporated both ducks and geese into his recipe with very interesting and extremely satisfying results.

Slice half a dozen duck breasts or two to three goose breast fillets into small strips or fingers, and set aside. Pour a 20-ounce jar of ordinary yellow mustard into a mixing bowl. Add finely-ground pure cayenne pepper –

The preparation of Duck 'ala Orange (Pop) in mid-stride.

The author's wife and gunning companion, Julie, prepares to serve her rendition of Duck ála Orange.

yes, cayenne pepper – until the mustard noticeably changes from yellow to a reddish-orange color. Dredge the duck or goose strips in the mustard, wipe the excess off on the edge of the bowl, and roll in Zatarain's New Orleans Fish Fry batter. Once you have a pile, as Bagley calls it, of strips breaded, deep-fat fry them in either peanut or canola oil, and drain. Serve with a fresh green salad, Ken's Italian dressing, wild rice, and lots and lots of ice water, tea, milk, or beer. Is it hot? You bet. Hot enough to the point where Bagley, upon introducing the recipe, made the statement in one e-mail message – "It's probably going to be too hot for you Yankees." Truth is, he was damn near right.

Duck ála Orange (Pop)

My wife got this suggestion from a friend, and then, as she's prone to do, twisted and tweaked it to the point of culinary perfection. With my apologies to the French, we call it Duck ála Orange Pop.

To a one-liter bottle of orange soda pop, add garlic oil (or pieces of fresh garlic), salt, pepper, and a tablespoon of sugar. Those who enjoy a little bit of heat – that's me – might want to add a few dashes of Chinese hot sesame oil or some chili-based oil to the bottle. Shake the pop gently until mixed, open slowly and carefully, and pour the mixture into a glass bowl until three or four whole birds are completely immersed. Cover the bowl with plastic wrap and refrigerate overnight. The next day, line the birds, breast-down, in a roasting pan to which a little of the marinade has been added. Cover the pan tightly with a double layer of heavy-duty aluminum foil, and bake in a 375-degree oven for just slightly less than two hours. For something even more special, place apple slices, and small chunks of lemon, orange, and sweet onion into the birds prior to baking.

The end result. Isn't it what we're all looking for … really?

Decoy lessons. Hunters need to do more of this type of education in order to ensure the continuation of the waterfowling tradition.

Here, members of the U.S. Fish and Wildlife Service entertain and educate a contingent of young up-and-comers as part of a Youth Waterfowl Hunting Day in Washington. Are you doing your part?

14
The Future

The future of duck hunting in the United States is held not by powerful corporations, high-ranking politicians, or million-member conservation organizations. Certainly, these factions help, and have done just that remarkably well over the past 100 years. Still, the fact remains that all this might and influence aside, the future of duck hunting as we know it today is not in big hands, but in small hands. In hands not yet born. For the future of waterfowling, you see, rests in the hands of the next generation.

Our goal – no, our responsibility –as waterfowlers is to ensure that there in fact *is* a next generation, one with whom we feel comfortable entrusting that which we hold most dear. Today in the United States, the recruitment of young hunters into the fold is at an all-time low. Time, money, an increase in single-parent households, the economy, computer games. They all play a role in this most disappointing and very alarming downward trend; however, we as hunters and waterfowlers do have the tools at our disposal to both halt this downslide *and* slam it into reverse. How?

This year, make a promise to yourself and to the waterfowling community to introduce at least one young person to the art of duck hunting. Speak to a 4-H group. Take your retriever to your son's or daughter's school and give a demonstration. Teach duck calling to the local Boy or Girl Scouts. Volunteer to handle the duck hunting and identification segment of the next hunter education program in your county. Guides and outfitters, here's a challenge to you. If you don't

A father-son team watch a retriever demonstration during a waterfowl Youth Day at a western Washington refuge.

already, set aside one morning this season as a no-charge youth day. Don't know any kids who hunt ducks? A call to your local wildlife conservation officer or hunter education instructor will most likely find you with more than enough names and telephone numbers. Plan a lunch for the kids and their parents or guardians, explain what you'll be doing, provide all your credentials and background information, and let the adults ask questions. Then, take the kids hunting.

At no time in the hunter's history have the nation's young people been a more valuable resource than at present. We simply can't afford to ignore them. Nor should we. After all, someone got each one of us started. We should do at least that much for another generation of hunters.

Sure it takes time, but the investment will last a lifetime.

They're all puppies, aren't they? It's our job to raise them right.

Give a kid a duck and he'll be fascinated for an hour. Teach a kid to duck hunt, and he'll be hooked for life. *Photo courtesy of Mossy Oak.*

Former refuge manager Bruce Wiseman, a wonderful gentleman, duck hunter, and father who knows the importance of today's youth, demonstrates his quick-and-easy duck plucking methods.

What is the future of duck hunting in America? Only time will tell.

It's the grin that's the reward for knowing you've done a good job.

Manufacturers Listing:

Who's who in the world of waterfowling

Stuff, technically known as "gear" but which also can include information, advice, and criticism, is the thing with which waterfowler's are made. Below is a list of companies involved in the outdoor industry, many of whom deal in gear and gadgets designed specifically for the duck hunter.

Hunter's Specialties – calls, camo, accessories, videos
Buck Gardner Calls
6000 Huntington Ct. NE
Cedar Rapids, IA 52402
319-395-0321 – *www.hunterspec.com*

Phil Robertson – calls, accessories, videos
Duck Commander Products
3117 N. 7th St.
West Monroe, LA 71291
877-396-7612 – *www.duckcommander.com*

Fred Zink, Zink Outdoors – fine duck/goose calls, accessories, videos
9132 Barnes Rd.
Clayton, OH 45315
937-832-3436

Joe and Phil Volz
ATTBAR, Inc. (The AquaPod Folks)
5985 S. 6th Way
Ridgefield, WA 98642
360-887-3580 – *www.attbar.com*

Bill Jordan's Realtree – camouflage and accessories
Realtree Outdoor Products
1390 Box Circle
Columbus, GA 31907
www.realtree.com

Bug-Out Outdoorwear – anti-insect clothing
901 E. Stewart
Centerville, IA 52544
515-437-1936 – *www.bug-out-outdoorwear.com*

DeLorme Mapping – Atlas & Gazetteer series, CD maps
Two DeLorme Drive
Yarmouth, ME 04096
207-846-7000 – *www.delorme.com*

Flambeau Products – decoys and accessories
15981 Valplast Rd.
Middlefield, OH 44062
440-632-1631 – *www.flambeau.com*

Tim and Hunter Grounds – fine goose calls, videos
1414 Barnham Rd.
Johnston City, IL 62951
618-983-5649 – *www.timgrounds.com*

Final Approach, Inc. – Eliminator blinds, accessories, videos
1877 Hubbard Lane
Grants Pass, OR 97527
541-476-7562 – *www.finalapproachblinds.com*

Avery – boat blinds, camo, accessories
PO Box 240663
Memphis, TN 38124
800-333-5119 – *www.averyoutdoors.com*

Rocky Shoes & Boots, Inc. – waders, boots
39 E. Canal St.
Nelsonville, OH 45764
740-753-1951 – *www.rockyboots.com*

Remington Arms Company – shotguns and ammunition
870 Remington Dr.
Madison, NC 27025
www.remington.com

Winchester, Olin Corporation – ammunition and components
Olin Corp., Winchester Division
427 N. Shamrock St.
East Alton, IL 62024
618-258-3568 – *www.winchester.com*

Mossy Oak – camouflage, videos, accessories
Haas Outdoors Inc.
PO Box 757
West Point, MS 39773
800-331-5624 – *www.mossyoak.com*

USA Outdoors – youth outdoor education programs
Brad Petersen, CEO
1245 E. Fremont Circle S.
Littleton, CO 80122
303-795-2492

Tony Toye – waterfowl guide/Mississippi River
Big River Guide Service
43605 CTH E
Boscobel, WI 53805
608-375-7447

Outland Sports – Feather Flex decoys, Lohman calls, Big River Game Calls, videos, accessories
4500 Doniphan Dr.
Neosho, MO 64850
417-451-4438 – *www.outland-sports.com*

Bass Pro Shops – one-stop shopping for everything waterfowl
2500 E. Kearney
Springfield, MO 65898
1-800-BASS-PRO - *www.basspro.com*

Cabela's Inc. – you name it, they have it
One Cabela Dr.
Sidney, NE 69160
1-800-237-4444 – *www.cabelas.com*

Coyote Co. Leather – fine lanyards, gamestraps, accessories
3706 Yaupon Dr.
Grand Prairie, TX 75052
972-262-2050

Browning/U.S. Repeating Arms – shotguns, gun cases, clothing, accessories
One Browning Place
Morgan, UT 84050
800-333-3288 – *www.browning.com*

Outlaw Decoys Inc. – decoys, boats, and accessories
624 N. Fancher Rd.
Spokane, WA 99212
1-800-OUTLAWS – *www.outlaw.com*